THE NO-COOK
COOKBOOK

RECIPES BY
REBECCA WOOLLARD

DK

DK | Penguin Random House

Author Rebecca Woollard

Editor Katie Lawrence
Project art editor Charlotte Bull
Designer Charlotte Jennings
US Editor Margaret Parrish
US Executive editor Lori Hand
US Senior editor Shannon Beatty
Food stylist and home economist Denise Smart
Photographer Ruth Jenkinson
Recipe tester Jessica Meyer
Production editor Dragana Puvacic
Senior production controller Ena Matagic
Jacket designer Charlotte Bull
Jacket co-ordinator Issy Walsh
Managing editor Jonathan Melmoth
Managing art editor Diane Peyton Jones
Publishing manager Francesca Young
Creative director Helen Senior
Publishing director Sarah Larter

First American Edition, 2021
Published in the United States by DK Publishing
1450 Broadway, Suite 801, New York, NY 10018

Copyright © 2021 Dorling Kindersley Limited
DK, a Division of Penguin Random House LLC
21 22 23 24 25 10 9 8 7 6 5 4 3 2 1
001-321062-Mar/2021

A catalog record for this book
is available from the Library of Congress.
ISBN: 978-0-7440-2646-7

DK books are available at special discounts when
purchased in bulk for sales promotions, premiums,
fund-raising, or educational use. For details, contact:
DK Publishing Special Markets,
1450 Broadway, Suite 801, New York, NY 10018
SpecialSales@dk.com

Printed and bound in China

For the curious
www.dk.com

This book was made with Forest Stewardship
Council ™ certified paper—one small step
in DK's commitment to a sustainable future.

For more information go to
www.dk.com/our-green-pledge

CONTENTS

4-5 How the book works

6-7 Kitchen rules

8-9 Tools

10-11 Gardening equipment

12-19 Techniques

20-21 No-bake granola

22-23 Overnight oatmeal

24-27 Breakfast smoothies

28-29 Grow your own tomatoes

30-31 Muffuletta

32-33 Nectarine and feta salad

34-35 Avocado spread

36-37 Chickpea and tomato salad

38-39 Grow your own lettuce

40-41 Picnic baguettes

42-43 Mint pea soup

44-45 Cauliflower rice bowl

46-47 Chopped salad

48-49 Chicken Caesar salad

50-51 Gazpacho

52-53 Couscous and spinach salad

54-55 Grow your own carrots

56-57 Dip pots

58-59 Indian sharing platter

60-61 Crepe spirals

62-63 Fruit and cheese skewers

64-65 Nutty red bell pepper puree

66-67 Dukkah and labneh

68-69 Almond butter dip

70-71 Soaked olives

72-73 Grow your own spinach

74-75 Smoked fish pâté

76-77 Shrimp butter pots

78-81 Zucchini noodles

82-83 Shrimp summer rolls

84-85 Coleslaw three ways

86-87 Sweet mustard and dill sauce

88-89 Panzanella

90-91 Taco feast

92-93 Seafood hand rolls

94-95 Chicken and mango boats

96-97 Raw pizza

98-99 Zucchini and tuna salad

100-101 Grow your own strawberries

102-103 Fruit parfaits

104-105 Chocolate power balls

106-107 Raspberry ripple fridge cake

108-109 Mini trifles

110-111 Watermelon slush

112-113 Black Forest banana splits

114-115 Apple doughnuts

116-119 No-bake crumbles

120-123 Semifreddos

124-125 Glossary

126-127 Index

128 Acknowledgments

HOW THE BOOK WORKS

This cookbook will help you to become more independent in the kitchen. It's packed full of delicious meals, top tips for food storage, and instructions for growing your own fruits and vegetables.

"Tip" suggestions help you make a recipe or tell you how to store the finished creation.

RECIPES

Follow the recipe steps to learn how to whip up each and every dish in this cookbook.

This is the list of ingredients you'll need for a recipe.

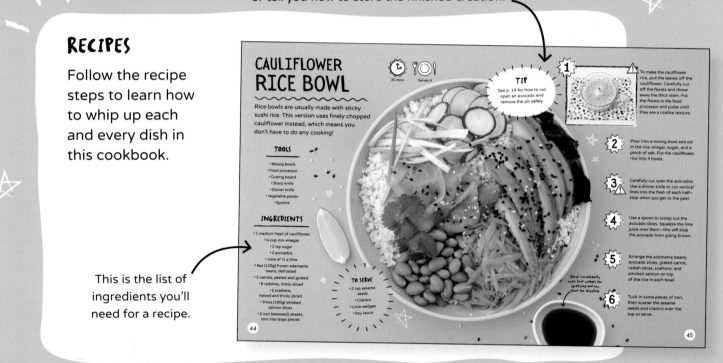

RECIPE VARIATIONS

Some pages have different types of the same recipe on them.

Look for "Change it up!" circles—they'll tell you extra ways to make a recipe.

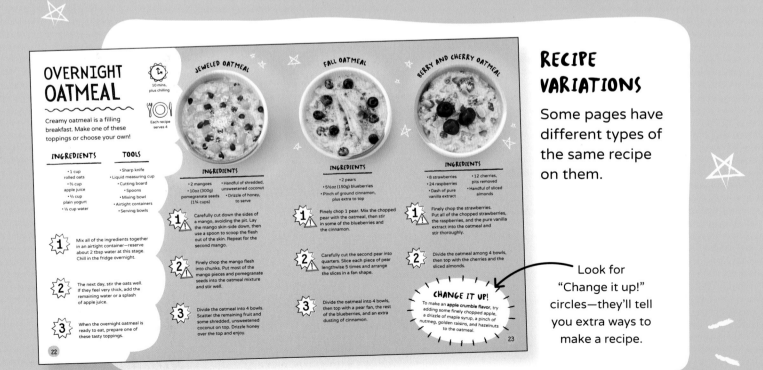

Each recipe is broken down into steps.

FOLLOW-ON RECIPES

The recipes on these pages follow on from the previous page. They show you even more suggestions for different recipe variations.

SPINACH PESTO

10 mins, plus marinating · Serves 4

TOOLS
- Cutting board
- Sharp knife
- Mixing bowl
- Spoons

INGREDIENTS
- 4oz (120g) feta cheese
- 1¼lb (500g) tomatoes, coarsely chopped
- 2 tsp red wine vinegar
- Large pinch of sugar
- 2 tbsp extra virgin olive oil, plus extra to serve
- Zucchini noodles (p. 78)
- 1 tsp dried oregano

1. Use your hands to break the feta cheese into chunks and set aside. Put the tomatoes, vinegar, sugar, olive oil, and a pinch of salt in the mixing bowl.

2. Stir everything together, then let soak for 15–20 minutes so that the tomatoes soften and release tasty juices into the bowl.

3. Add the zucchini noodles to the mixing bowl and toss together with the tomato mixture. Stir in the feta cheese chunks and oregano. Divide among 4 bowls, then twist it all up and eat!

SPINACH PESTO

10 mins · Serves 4

TOOLS
- Food processor
- Mixing bowl
- Spoons
- Garlic press

INGREDIENTS
- 3½oz (100g) spinach leaves
- 1½ cups fresh basil leaves, plus extra to serve
- ½ cup pine nuts
- 1 garlic clove, crushed
- 3 tbsp olive oil
- 1¾oz (50g) Parmesan cheese, grated, plus extra to serve
- Zucchini noodles (p. 78)

1. Put all of the ingredients, except for the noodles, into the food processor with a generous helping of salt and freshly ground pepper. Pulse until the pesto is smooth.

2. Place the zucchini noodles in the mixing bowl and spoon in the pesto. Use your hands to coat the noodles.

3. Divide among 4 bowls and top with some basil leaves and a little more grated Parmesan—add as much as you like.

81

ZUCCHINI NOODLES

Use a spiralizer to make zucchini noodles that look very similar to spaghetti. But unlike spaghetti, zucchini noodles don't need to be cooked—just add a tasty sauce and enjoy a healthy dinner.

20 mins · Serves 4

TOOLS
- Cutting board
- Sharp knife
- Spiralizer
- Scissors

FOR THE ZUCCHINI NOODLES
- 4 zucchini, halved with ends trimmed

1. See p. 14 for how to use a spiralizer. Take extra care when using one—they can be quite sharp. Use it to cut the zucchini—you should end up with a big tangle of noodles. Repeat for the remaining zucchini.

2. If the noodles are longer than normal spaghetti, use scissors to trim them. Use the zucchini as soon as you've spiralized it—it doesn't keep very well and can become soft.

3. Choose one of the three sauces on this page or the next, coat the zucchini noodles, twirl them around your fork, then enjoy!

CHANGE IT UP!
If you don't have a spiralizer, a julienne peeler is a great alternative and will produce thin zucchini noodles.

78

CREAMY AVOCADO AND PARMESAN

5 mins · Serves 4

TO SERVE
- Small mint leaves
- Sprinkle of chili flakes

TOOLS
- Cutting board
- Sharp knife
- Food processor
- Mixing bowl
- Garlic press
- Microplane
- Spoons

INGREDIENTS
- 2 ripe avocados
- 1½oz (40g) Parmesan cheese, grated, plus extra to serve
- Juice of 1 lemon, plus the grated zest to serve
- 1 garlic clove, crushed
- 2 tbsp extra virgin olive oil, plus extra to serve
- Zucchini noodles

1. See p. 14 for how to cut open an avocado and remove the pit. Repeat for the second avocado.

2. Using a spoon, scoop the flesh out from each avocado half, then put it in the food processor. Add the Parmesan cheese, lemon juice, crushed garlic, olive oil, and a pinch of salt.

3. Pulse everything until it's completely smooth, then taste and add more salt if you think the recipe needs it.

4. Put the zucchini in a bowl and pour the sauce over the top. Using your hands, toss everything together until the noodles are completely coated in the sauce. It might be messy work, but it's worth it!

5. Divide among 4 bowls. Top with some lemon zest, a few mint leaves, chili flakes, if you can handle the spice, and, finally, a drizzle of olive oil.

This tells you how to present the dish.

When you see this symbol, turn to the next page to see more variations of the same recipe.

This is the list of tools you'll need.

Photos show you what the plant should look like at each stage.

GROW YOUR OWN TOMATOES

Grow in a sunny place · Plant in spring

Here's how to grow tasty tomatoes bursting with flavor—the type shown here are called "Sweet 100." Plant these cherry tomatoes somewhere that gets lots of light.

TOOLS
- Containers
- Seed potting mix
- Tomato seeds
- Large container with holes
- All-purpose compost

1. Use seed potting mix to fill a container. Add the tomato seeds, then cover with more seed potting mix. Keep in a warm place, water well, and when you see leaves sprout, move to somewhere sunny.

2. Wait until 2 or 3 tomato plants have sprouted. Then take your large container with holes and fill it with all-purpose compost. Add your tomato plants and cover the roots with more compost.

3. Place in a sunny position and keep your tomato plants well watered to help them grow. Wash them before eating.

TIP
Use your tomatoes in these recipes.

29

GROW YOUR OWN

Learn how to grow your own fruits and vegetables on these pages. See p. 10 for all the tools you'll need.

Here are some of the recipes you can make using the ingredient you have grown.

KITCHEN RULES

Even though cooking can get a little messy, it's important to always think about cleanliness and safety while following each recipe. Read through all of these rules before getting started.

BE CAREFUL

This symbol means you're about to use something sharp or electrical. Take extra care or ask an adult for help.

TOOLS AND INGREDIENTS

Before you start on a recipe, make sure you have all the tools you need. You might need to borrow some or buy something new.

✦ Get all the ingredients ready. You may have some at home, but you may need to buy others.

✦ For recipes in this book, it's best to use large-sized eggs.

✦ Use whole, low-fat, skim, or plant-based milk for recipes that require milk.

WEIGHTS AND MEASUREMENTS

Measure any ingredients you need before you start. Use tablespoons, teaspoons, scales, and a liquid measuring cup, as needed. Here's a guide to the abbreviations used in this cookbook:

METRIC

g = gram
kg = kilogram
ml = milliliter
l = liter

US STANDARD

oz = ounce
lb = pound
fl oz = fluid ounce

GETTING STARTED

✦ Read the recipe all the way through before you begin.

✦ Roll up your sleeves, tie back long hair, and put on your favorite apron.

✦ Chop or slice anything that needs it.

SPOON MEASURES

tsp = teaspoon
tbsp = tablespoon

KITCHEN SAFETY

Make sure you enjoy yourself in the kitchen—but remember that safety comes first. Follow these steps so that you don't hurt yourself. If you're not sure about anything, ask an adult to help.

- Be extra careful when peeling, grating, cutting, spiralizing, or using anything electrical.
- Be very careful when cutting a large fruit or vegetable that has a thick rind, such as a watermelon. Cut it into quarters first, then cut off the rind before chopping into chunks.
- Ask an adult for help if you don't feel confident or comfortable using a sharp knife.
- Wipe up any spills and clean up as you go.
- Don't put your hands near the moving parts of an electrical tool, such as a food processor, unless you're absolutely certain it's switched off at the outlet.
- Wash your hands after handling anything spicy, such as chili flakes, and avoid touching your mouth, eyes, or other sensitive areas.

SERVING SIZE

This tells you the final amount or the number of portions a recipe makes, or how many people it serves.

20 mins   Makes 4–6

PREPARATION TIME

This is how long a recipe will take to complete. It also tells you if you need to allow extra time for additional preparation, such as freezing or chilling.

KITCHEN HYGIENE

Follow these rules to prevent germs from spreading and to stop you from getting sick.

- Wash your hands before you start preparing food.
- Wash all fruits and vegetables before using.
- Use hot, soapy water to clean cutting boards between each use.
- Check the use-by date on all ingredients.
- Make sure the area where you are preparing food is kept clean.
- Wash your hands after handling raw eggs.
- Please note that the Sweet mustard and dill sauce and the Semifreddos contain egg that isn't fully cooked. Don't serve these dishes to an elderly person, a baby, or a pregnant woman.

Plastic wrap

Foil

Parchment paper

Kitchen scissors

Serrated knife

Bread knife

Sharp knife

Dinner knife

Fork

Metal spoon

Salad servers

Wooden spoon

Whisk

Spatula

TOOLS

Here are all of the tools used in this cookbook. Make sure you have the ones you need on hand before starting a recipe.

Serving glasses

Box grater

Kitchen twine

Ramekins

Juicer

Toothpicks

Ice-pop sticks

Cheesecloth

Frying pan

Apple corer

Ice-cream scoop

Pizza cutter

Microplane

Dish towel

Sieve

You'll need this to weigh down the Muffuletta on pp. 30–31.

Mixing bowls

Serving bowls

Liquid measuring cup

Measuring cups

Mortar and pestle

Kitchen scales

These clip-top jars work well as airtight containers.

Airtight containers

Can opener

Garlic press

Measuring spoons

Spiralizer

See the guide on p. 14 for how to use this.

Julienne peeler

Vegetable peeler

Serving dish

Freezer bags

Freezer-proof container

Ice-pop molds

These are just one type of ice-pop mold you could use.

Loaf pan

Cutting board

Baking sheet

Rolling pin

Food processor

Small food processor

Blender

Electric mixer

Paper towels

9

GARDENING EQUIPMENT

To grow the fruits and vegetables in this book, you'll need these handy pieces of equipment.

GETTING STARTED

Make sure you have the correct equipment before planting your seeds. Read the instructions through completely, so you know what you'll need for every stage.

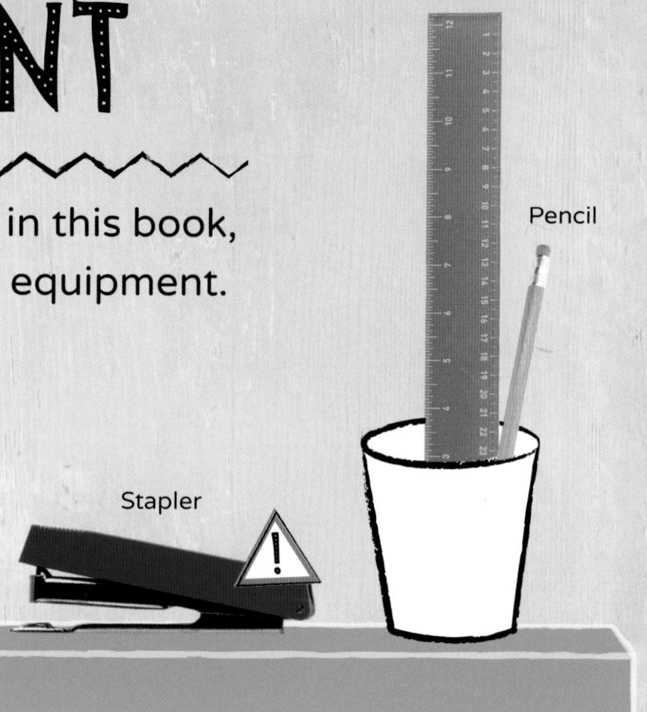

Ruler

Pencil

Stapler

Scissors

Burlap bag

Trash bag

Plant pots

Strawberry plug

Liquid fertilizer

Straw

Gravel

Soil

Potting mix

WHEN TO PLANT

Look for this symbol on each of the Grow Your Own pages—it will tell you the best time of year to start planting.

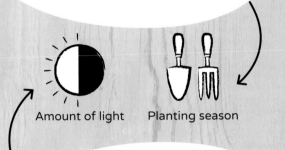

Amount of light   Planting season

WHERE TO GROW

This symbol tells you how much light each plant needs. All of the plants in this book can be grown in a garden, on a windowsill, or on a balcony.

Seeds

Large container with drainage holes

Seed potting mix

All-purpose compost

WHAT PLANTS NEED TO GROW

All plants need to be cared for to thrive. Different plants grow best in different conditions, but here are some general tips.

Time
All plants need time to grow. It might take a while for them to sprout leaves—so you have to be patient with them!

Temperature
Some plants, such as sunflowers, grow best in warm temperatures, while others like to be kept cool. Make sure you keep your plants at the temperature they prefer.

Water, air, and light
Plants need energy from food to grow. This energy is made in a process called photosynthesis. Plants use carbon dioxide gas from the air, water, and light from the sun to create their food.

Soil
Soil acts as an anchor for plants—it keeps their roots steady and secure while they grow. It also behaves like a sponge, absorbing water for the plant to soak up.

TECHNIQUES

〜〜〜〜〜〜〜〜〜〜〜〜〜

Every good cook has to master these basic techniques. They'll help you to prepare dishes easily and safely.

PEELERS

VEGETABLE PEELER

This is used not only to peel vegetables, such as carrots, but also to make crunchy vegetable ribbons. Remember to keep your fingers tucked away when peeling!

JULIENNE PEELER

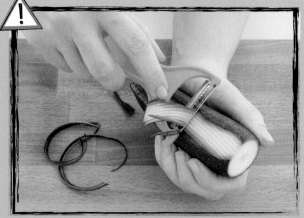

This is like a vegetable peeler, but it has little teeth instead of a flat blade. When used, the teeth drag down through vegetables to create very thin strips.

1 To make vegetable ribbons and julienne strips, hold the vegetable firmly at an angle. If using carrots, peel them first.

Carrot ribbons

Julienned zucchini

2 Drag the peeler downward, giving the vegetable a quarter turn every three peels, so it peels evenly. Stop when you get to seeds or the central core.

SHARP KNIFE

A sharp knife is usually safer to use than a blunt one, and it's an essential tool for any kitchen. Keep your knives sharp by handwashing and drying them as soon as you've finished using them. Never leave sharp knives in a sink full of water, since someone could put their hand in and cut themselves.

HOW TO HOLD A KNIFE

Put a piece of damp paper towel under the cutting board. This will stop the board from slipping.

Grip the knife's handle firmly with the hand you write with. Your thumb and forefinger should rest on the top of the handle where it meets the blade.

BRIDGE TECHNIQUE

Hold big vegetables between your thumb and forefinger, making a bridge. Carefully cut down under the bridge.

CLAW TECHNIQUE

Tuck your fingertips in like a claw when slicing food. Even if your knife slips, it won't harm your hand.

Chop Try to chop the food into about ½–1 in (1–2 cm) wide pieces.

Finely chop Try to get the pieces as small as possible, roughly ¼ in (0.5 cm) wide.

Dice If the recipe says to cube or dice, cut the food evenly in ½ in (1 cm) cubes.

Snip Herbs can be sliced any way you like. It's even easier to use scissors!

REMOVING AVOCADO PITS

1 Rest the avocado on a cutting board and use the claw technique to hold it with one hand. Use a small knife to cut all the way around the avocado until you feel the knife hit the pit.

2 Hold the top and bottom of the avocado with each hand. Gently twist the avocado halves to separate them.

3 Pull the two halves away from each other. Put the half without the pit to one side.

4 Use a spoon to scoop out the pit from the remaining half and throw it away.

SPIRALIZER

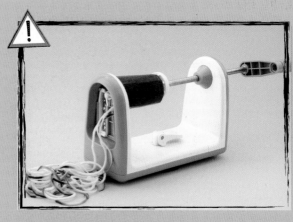

If you don't have a spiralizer, you can use a julienne peeler to get a similar effect.

Spiralizers come in many shapes and sizes, but they all do the same job: turning firm vegetables, such as zucchini, into long, noodle-shaped spirals. Follow the instructions on the spiralizer you have. Be extra careful when using one, as they can be quite sharp.

BOX GRATER

A box grater has four different sides. Put it on a cutting board and hold the handle while you're working—this will keep the grater secure. Always grate down and away from your body, and watch your fingers!

TIP
Keep your grater sharp by washing it by hand only. Blunt graters can cause accidents.

LARGE GRATER

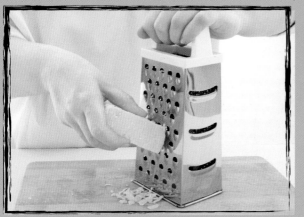

This is best for cheese, cucumber, and anything else you want in large pieces. If a recipe asks for something to be grated, this is the side to use.

SMALL GRATER

This side is great for Parmesan, ginger, and garlic. It produces small pieces of the food. If a recipe step needs you to grate something finely, use this side.

ZESTER
The small holes with raised teeth are used for zesting fruit. This side is tricky to use, however, and not very effective. We recommend using a microplane instead (see p. 17).

SLICER
You won't need this side for recipes in this book, but it can slice apples and potatoes. It's difficult to master, so if you want to try using it, ask an adult to help.

SEPARATING EGG YOLKS AND WHITES

1

Crack the egg gently on a flat surface or the side of a bowl. Hold it upright and carefully prize the shell into halves—keep the contents of the egg in one half of the shell.

2

Hold the egg over a bowl and gently pour the yolk between the halves, so that the egg white drips into the bowl. Once the white is gone, put the yolk into another bowl.

BEATING

HAND WHISK

When using a hand whisk, it helps to tilt the bowl you're using slightly and to whisk quickly and confidently.

ELECTRIC MIXER

Hold the bowl and slowly move the beaters while keeping them firmly in the mixture. It works quickly, so be careful not to overbeat.

JUICING CITRUS FRUIT

Using a juicer
Cut the fruit in half, then push it onto the tip of the juicer flesh-first. Twist the fruit around the tip and keep pushing down to release its tasty juice.

Juicing by hand
Slice the fruit in half. Use one hand to squeeze it over a bowl. Cup your other hand under the fruit—the juice will run through your fingers, but you'll catch the seeds.

FOLDING

Folding is a way of mixing two ingredients together without knocking the air out. Use a large metal spoon in a gentle figure-eight motion and slowly rotate the bowl so everything is mixed evenly. Always fold the thinner substance into the thicker one, not the other way around.

ZESTING WITH A MICROPLANE

Rest the microplane on a cutting board and hold it at an angle. To zest, carefully rub the fruit over the microplane. Every so often, scrape the back of the microplane with a teaspoon to clear any zest that is stuck.

You can use a microplane to grate ginger finely, too.

When zesting citrus fruit, stop when you get to the white pith under the skin. This tastes bitter and will spoil the food.

CRUSHING GARLIC

1 Put the garlic clove on a cutting board and carefully press down on it with the flat side of a knife. Once the skin has broken, it should peel off easily.

2 Trim the ends off the garlic clove, then put it in a garlic press. Squeeze the garlic press with both hands over a bowl. Use a teaspoon to scrape off any garlic that is stuck.

USING HERBS

Fresh herbs make food taste really flavorful.

TIP
Don't skimp on fresh herbs! Not only do they taste good, but they also look beautiful—especially fresh, soft herbs such as basil, mint, and cilantro.

BASIL

If you're picking herbs from a plant, gently take from the top leaves and stems. Be careful not to bruise or damage the rest of the plant. This will encourage new leaves to grow.

COOKING INDEPENDENTLY

FOLLOWING RECIPES

Before you start cooking, read the recipe through completely so you know what you'll be doing. This should prevent you from forgetting any tools, ingredients, or steps you will need. If you have time, clean up as you go—it will save you from having a big cleanup job at the end and will keep your kitchen nice and neat.

COOKING WITHOUT HEAT

Because these recipes don't use heat, they're easy to manage without an adult. Of course, if you're not sure about anything or need help with knife tasks, ask an adult. But, if you're careful and confident to do it alone, you can make most of the recipes from start to finish by yourself.

TRYING NEW THINGS

We've used many ingredients in this book—some you'll be familiar with and others you might not be. It's important to be brave—you might end up not liking something, but that means you'll know for the next time! Having an open mind about trying new things is a great life skill to learn.

NO-BAKE GRANOLA

This breakfast food is usually baked, but this no-cook version still gives you the same fantastic flavors.

10 mins

Makes about 3½ cups

TOOLS

• Mixing bowl
• Spoons
• Airtight container

INGREDIENTS

• 1 cup unsweetened oats with large toasted flakes
• ½ cup dried, toasted coconut flakes
• ⅓ cup toasted, sliced almonds
• ⅓ cup golden raisins
• ¼ cup roasted, chopped hazelnuts

TO SERVE

• Maple syrup
• Handful of fresh fruit
• 2–3 tbsp plain yogurt

1 To make the granola, just mix all the dry ingredients together. Keep it in an airtight container, somewhere cool and dry.

2 When ready to eat, measure out a 1½oz (40g) portion of granola—about ⅓ cup. Stir in 1 tsp of maple syrup, then top with fresh fruit and plain yogurt.

OVERNIGHT OATMEAL

10 mins, plus chilling

Each recipe serves 4

Creamy oatmeal is a filling breakfast. Make one of these toppings or choose your own!

INGREDIENTS

- 1 cup rolled oats
- $\frac{2}{3}$ cup apple juice
- $\frac{2}{3}$ cup plain yogurt
- $\frac{1}{2}$ cup water

TOOLS

- Sharp knife
- Liquid measuring cup
- Cutting board
- Spoons
- Mixing bowl
- Airtight containers
- Serving bowls

 1 Mix all of the ingredients together in an airtight container—reserve about 2 tbsp water at this stage. Chill in the fridge overnight.

 2 The next day, stir the oats well. If they feel very thick, add the remaining water or a splash of apple juice.

 3 When the overnight oatmeal is ready to eat, prepare one of these tasty toppings.

JEWELED OATMEAL

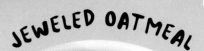

INGREDIENTS

- 2 mangoes
- 10oz (300g) pomegranate seeds (1¾ cups)
- Handful of shredded, unsweetened coconut
- Drizzle of honey, to serve

 1 ⚠ Carefully cut down the sides of a mango, avoiding the pit. Lay the mango skin-side down, then use a spoon to scoop the flesh out of the skin. Repeat for the second mango.

2 ⚠ Finely chop the mango flesh into chunks. Put most of the mango pieces and pomegranate seeds into the oatmeal mixture and stir well.

 3 Divide the oatmeal into 4 bowls. Scatter the remaining fruit and some shredded, unsweetened coconut on top. Drizzle honey over the top and enjoy.

FALL OATMEAL

BERRY AND CHERRY OATMEAL

INGREDIENTS

- 2 pears
- 5½oz (150g) blueberries
- Pinch of ground cinnamon, plus extra to top

INGREDIENTS

- 8 strawberries
- 24 raspberries
- Dash of pure vanilla extract
- 12 cherries, pits removed
- Handful of sliced almonds

 Finely chop 1 pear. Mix the chopped pear with the oatmeal, then stir in some of the blueberries and the cinnamon.

 Finely chop the strawberries. Put all of the chopped strawberries, the raspberries, and the pure vanilla extract into the oatmeal and stir thoroughly.

 Carefully cut the second pear into quarters. Slice each piece of pear lengthwise 5 times and arrange the slices in a fan shape.

 Divide the oatmeal among 4 bowls, then top with the cherries and the sliced almonds.

 Divide the oatmeal into 4 bowls, then top with a pear fan, the rest of the blueberries, and an extra dusting of cinnamon.

CHANGE IT UP!
To make an **apple crumble flavor**, try adding some finely chopped apple, a drizzle of maple syrup, a pinch of nutmeg, golden raisins, and hazelnuts to the oatmeal.

BREAKFAST SMOOTHIES

Almost everyone loves smoothies! They are full of fresh fruits and vegetables. Here are 5 flavors to try…

INGREDIENTS

- 3½oz (100g) spinach
- 1 banana, peeled and coarsely chopped
- 4 dates, pits removed
- ⅓ cup roasted, chopped hazelnuts
- 1 cup apple juice
- 2 pears, coarsely chopped

INGREDIENTS

- 10oz (300g) frozen mixed berries
- ⅔ cup unsweetened rolled oats
- 1 cup milk
- ½–1 tbsp maple syrup
- Juice of ½ a lemon

GREEN GOODNESS

VERY BERRY

PB&J

TOOLS

- Spoons
- Scales
- Liquid measuring cup
- Blender
- Cutting board
- Sharp knife
- Paper straws
- Mixing bowl

1 Put the mixing bowl on the scales and reset the scales to zero. Weigh the ingredients in the bowl, resetting the scales to zero each time you add a new ingredient.

2 Measure anything you can't weigh separately, such as milk or juice, then pour all of the ingredients into the blender. Puree everything together until there are no lumps.

3 If your blender has trouble pureeing any fruit, add a little more milk, water, or juice. Pour into glasses and serve with a paper straw.

INGREDIENTS

- 10oz (300g) raspberries
- ¼ cup peanut butter
- 1 cup orange juice
- 1 tbsp honey
- 1 banana, peeled and coarsely chopped

INGREDIENTS

- 5½oz (150g) strawberries
- 5½oz (150g) mango chunks
- 1 cup orange juice
- 1 banana, peeled and coarsely chopped
- 1 tsp honey

INGREDIENTS

- 1¾oz (50g) sachet of creamed coconut
- 10oz (300g) pineapple chunks
- 1 cup milk
- 1 banana, peeled and coarsely chopped

TIP

These smoothies will keep covered in the fridge for up to 2 days. Stir them well before serving.

SUNSET SMOOTHIE

TOTALLY TROPICAL

Once you're an expert at making smoothies, try out these different ways to serve them.

20 mins, plus freezing

Makes 4

TOOLS

- Spoons
- Cutting board
- Sharp knife
- Food processor

SMOOTHIE BOWLS

1 Choose any smoothie flavor from pp. 24–25.

2 Before you start, freeze any fruit that's needed for up to 12 hours.

3 Once the fruit is frozen, put it into the food processor with the other ingredients. Use about ¼ cup less fruit juice or milk than in the smoothie recipe, since the mixture needs to be nice and thick.

4 Blend everything together in the food processor. ⚠

5 Pour the mixture into 4 bowls, then decorate with your choice of toppings—try fresh fruit, nuts, seeds, shredded coconut, chocolate chips, or even edible flowers!

SMOOTHIE POPS

15 mins,
plus freezing

Makes 18

TOOLS

- Pitcher
- 3fl oz (90ml) capacity ice-pop molds
- Ice-pop sticks
- Freezer-proof containers

1 Choose any 3 smoothie flavors from pp. 24–25 and make them using the method on the same page.

2 Place each smoothie in the freezer for roughly 20 minutes, then transfer each smoothie to a pitcher. Pour them slowly, one after the other, into ice-pop molds. Be careful not to pour too quickly or the colors will run into each other.

3 Put the ice-pop sticks into the smoothie-filled molds, then freeze for at least 6 hours, or for up to 1 week.

4 When the smoothie pops are frozen and ready to eat, run each mold under warm water until you can pull the smoothie pop free.

TIP

You can also make smoothie pops with just 1 smoothie flavor. You'll end up with 6 pops instead of 18, and you won't need to freeze the smoothie before pouring it into the molds.

Grow in a
sunny place

Plant in
spring

GROW YOUR OWN
TOMATOES

Here's how to grow tasty tomatoes bursting with flavor—the type shown here are called "Sweet 100." Plant these cherry tomatoes somewhere that gets lots of light.

TOOLS

- Containers
- Seed potting mix
- Tomato seeds
- Large container with holes
- All-purpose compost

1

2

3

Use seed potting mix to fill a container. Add the tomato seeds, then cover with more seed potting mix. Keep in a warm place, water well, and when you see leaves sprout, move to somewhere sunny.

Wait until 2 or 3 tomato plants have sprouted. Then take your large container with holes and fill it with all-purpose compost. Add your tomato plants and cover the roots with more compost.

Place in a sunny position and keep your tomato plants well watered to help them grow. Wash them before eating.

TIP

Use your tomatoes in these recipes.

Indian sharing Platter
PP. 58—59

Chickpea and tomato salad PP. 36—37

Avocado spread PP. 34—35

30 mins, plus resting

Serves 6–8

MUFFULETTA

This enormous round sandwich from New Orleans looks like a regular loaf of bread. When it's cut into wedges, however, you'll see layers and layers of colorful filling inside.

TOOLS

- Serrated knife
- Cutting board
- Small food processor
- Scales
- Teaspoon
- Plastic wrap
- Baking sheet
- Sieve
- Frying pan

INGREDIENTS

- 1 round Italian loaf or boule, about 7 in (18 cm) measured across the bottom
- 5½oz (150g) semi-dried tomatoes, drained
- ½ cup fresh basil pesto
- 7oz (200g) wafer-thin ham
- 5½oz (150g) smoked cheese slices
- 3½oz (100g) salami
- ¾ cup fresh basil
- 9oz (280g) roasted red bell peppers, drained and patted dry

1

Use the knife to cut off the top third of the loaf. Scoop out the insides with your hands, leaving a thin layer of bread inside.

2

Pulse the tomatoes to a paste in the food processor and set aside. Using the back of a teaspoon, spread the pesto inside the loaf and its lid, then repeat with the tomato paste.

3

At the bottom of the loaf, layer half of the ham, half of the cheese, and half the salami. Next, top with the basil leaves and all of the bell peppers. Finally, top with the remaining salami, cheese, and ham. Pack each layer in tightly and evenly.

4 Put the lid back on the loaf, then wrap in plastic and put on a baking sheet. Weigh down with a frying pan and transfer to the fridge for about 6 hours, or until the loaf has flattened slightly.

5 To serve, remove the plastic wrap, then carefully slice the loaf into wedges.

TIP
Keep the insides of the loaf to make Panzanella (see pp. 88–89).

20 mins

Serves 4

NECTARINE AND FETA SALAD

CHANGE IT UP!

You can swap out the nectarines for other fruits, such as cherries, peaches, or apples.

This colorful dish goes well with homemade honey mustard dressing. The almonds add some crunch—an essential part of any good salad!

TOOLS

- Jar with lid
- Sharp knife
- Cutting board
- Spoons
- Serving dish
- Salad servers
- Mortar and pestle

INGREDIENTS

- 3 nectarines
- 4oz (110g) salad greens
- 3½oz (100g) feta cheese
- Large handful of almonds

FOR THE DRESSING

- 1 tbsp whole-grain mustard
- 1 tbsp sherry vinegar or rice wine vinegar
- 2 tsp honey
- 3 tbsp olive oil

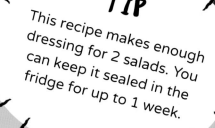

TIP
This recipe makes enough dressing for 2 salads. You can keep it sealed in the fridge for up to 1 week.

 1 To make the dressing, put the mustard, vinegar, and honey in the jar with a pinch of salt. Make sure the lid is screwed on tightly, then shake until everything is mixed together.

 2 Pour in the olive oil, then put the lid back on. Shake the jar again, until everything is combined and the dressing has thickened. Set aside.

 3 Use a sharp knife to carefully cut down each side of 1 nectarine until you're left with 4 large pieces and the pit. Cut each piece into thin slices and throw away the pit. Repeat for the remaining nectarines.

 4 Put the salad greens into the serving dish and top with the nectarine slices. Use your hands to crumble the feta cheese on top.

 5 Coarsely crush the almonds in the mortar and pestle. Scatter most of the crushed almonds into the serving dish.

 6 Drizzle about half of the dressing over the top and toss everything together with the salad servers. Sprinkle the rest of the almonds over the top, then enjoy!

33

10 mins Serves 1

AVOCADO SPREAD

This recipe can be made in minutes—it's perfect for a quick lunch. The smooth avocado and sweet pumpernickel bread will keep you feeling full all afternoon.

TOOLS

- Cutting board
- Bread knife
- Sharp knife
- Dinner knife
- Mixing bowl
- Vegetable peeler
- Fork
- Juicer
- Spoon

INGREDIENTS

- 1 small, ripe avocado
- Juice of ½ a lime
- 1 slice pumpernickel bread
- 1 medium tomato, sliced
- Parmesan cheese
- 6–8 small mint leaves, to serve
- Extra virgin olive oil, to serve

TIP

To check whether an avocado is ripe, squeeze it gently—it should feel a little bit soft. If it's still hard, it needs a few more days to ripen.

See p. 14 for how to cut open an avocado and remove the pit. Use a spoon to scoop out the avocado flesh, then put it in the mixing bowl.

 Squeeze the lime juice into the bowl and add a generous pinch of salt. Mash with a fork until most of the lumps are gone.

 Cut the slice of pumpernickel bread in half. Spread the mashed avocado over each half, then top with tomato slices.

 Use the vegetable peeler to peel some Parmesan shavings, then add those to the sandwich. Scatter mint leaves over the top and drizzle with a little olive oil. Gobble everything up immediately!

CHANGE IT UP!

Try using different flavored oils to drizzle over the top, such as garlic, chili, or basil. You can also use any type of bread you like.

If you've never had goat cheese, a soft one is a great place to start. It tastes a little like cream cheese, but with more of a tangy lemon flavor. It goes well with tomatoes.

CHICKPEA AND TOMATO SALAD

15 mins, plus marinating

Serves 4

TOOLS

- Serrated knife
- Can opener
- Cutting board
- Spoons
- Serving platter
- Salad servers
- Sieve
- Mortar and pestle

INGREDIENTS

- 10oz (300g) cherry tomatoes
- 2 tsp red wine vinegar
- ¼ tsp sugar
- 3 tbsp extra virgin olive oil
- 14oz (400g) can of chickpeas
- ½ tbsp cumin seeds
- ½ tbsp coriander seeds
- 2oz (50g) arugula
- 2½oz (75g) soft, rindless goat cheese

1 Carefully cut the cherry tomatoes in half. Put them on the serving platter with the red wine vinegar, sugar, olive oil, and a pinch of salt.

 2 Open the can of chickpeas and pour them into a sieve over a sink. Rinse well with cold water, then shake the sieve to get rid of extra water. Put onto the serving platter.

 3 Stir everything together and leave to marinate (soak together) for about 25 minutes. The tomato juices will begin to mix with the vinegar and oil.

 4 Gently crush the cumin and coriander seeds in the mortar and pestle. When you're ready to serve, add the arugula and spices to the serving platter.

5 Using your fingers, gently crumble the goat cheese over the top. Toss everything together using salad servers, then enjoy!

Grow in a
sunny place

Plant in spring
to summer

GROW YOUR OWN
LETTUCE

 1 Use the pencil to make a few holes roughly ½ in (1.5 cm) deep in a plant pot filled with seed potting mix. Sprinkle lettuce seeds in each hole. Cover with potting mix, then water.

2 Pull out some leaves once the lettuce plants start to sprout. Keep well watered.

3 To stop pesky slugs from eating the leaves, pour some gravel on the soil around the plant when it reaches roughly this size.

4

If the weather is warm, you'll need to water this plant once or twice a day. When you want to eat some lettuce, only pick the outer leaves off the plant. Wash and enjoy!

TIP

Use your lettuce
in these recipes.

Chopped salad
PP. 46—47

Seafood hand rolls
PP. 92—93

Coronation chicken
picnic baguette P. 47

Lettuce comes in many different varieties, so plant your favorite. Watch the leaves—they will keep growing and growing!

PICNIC BAGUETTES

20 mins

Each recipe serves 6–8

These sandwiches are packed with fantastic flavors and are great to make for a picnic. Take your pick from these fillings, or make them all!

INGREDIENTS

- 1 baguette
- 2 tbsp butter, softened

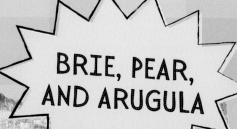

BRIE, PEAR, AND ARUGULA

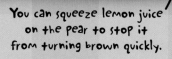

You can squeeze lemon juice on the pear to stop it from turning brown quickly.

INGREDIENTS

- 1–2 tbsp sweet chili sauce
- 7–10 slices of brie
- 10–12 slices of pear
- Large handful of arugula
- Juice of ½ a lemon (optional)

1 Spread the sweet chili sauce all along the baguette. Fill with slices of brie, pear, and arugula.

INGREDIENTS

- 3 tbsp mayonnaise
- 1½ tbsp ketchup
- 5–6 drops of Worcestershire sauce
- Juice of ½ a lemon
- 6oz (175g) cooked jumbo shrimp
- Handful of watercress
- Handful of prawn crackers, to serve

TOOLS

- Bread knife
- Dinner knife
- Parchment paper or aluminum foil
- Scissors
- Spoons
- Paper towels
- Mixing bowls

1 Carefully slice the baguette lengthwise three-quarters of the way through. Don't cut the baguette fully in half.

2 Spread butter along the baguette, then stuff with your choice of filling. Don't fill too full though, or ingredients will spill out!

3 Wrap the sandwich in foil or parchment paper and keep it in the fridge until you're ready for your picnic.

SHRIMP COCKTAIL

CORONATION CHICKEN

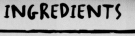

1 Put the mayonnaise, ketchup, Worcestershire sauce, and lemon juice in a bowl. Season with salt and pepper, then mix together.

2 Pat the shrimp dry with paper towels, then stir into the sauce. Put a layer of watercress along the baguette, then spoon in the shrimp mixture. Add prawn crackers for an extra crunch!

INGREDIENTS

- Handful of little gem lettuce leaves
- Handful of cucumber slices
- 9oz (250g) precooked chicken breasts, shredded
- 3 tbsp Greek yogurt
- 3 tbsp mayonnaise
- 1 tsp medium curry powder
- ¼ tsp turmeric
- 1 tbsp mango chutney
- 3 tsp finely chopped fresh mint

1 Line the baguette with the lettuce leaves and cucumber slices. Mix together the other ingredients, then fill the baguette and enjoy.

41

MINT PEA SOUP

This refreshing, bright green soup is perfect for hot days, as it is served cold!

10 mins

Serves 4

TOOLS

- Liquid measuring cup
- Blender
- Spoons
- Bowls

INGREDIENTS

- 14oz (400g) frozen peas, defrosted, plus extra to garnish
- 2 cups chicken stock
- 3½oz (100g) baguette, torn into small chunks, plus extra to serve
- 24 mint leaves
- Juice of 1 lemon
- 1 tbsp crème fraîche
- 4 precooked bacon strips, coarsely chopped (omit for vegetarians)
- Extra virgin olive oil, to drizzle

TIP

Try to use liquid stock so you don't have to boil water, but if you only have a bouillon cube, you can use that instead. Ask an adult to pour boiling water over the cube in a liquid measuring cup until you have 2 cups of stock. Stir until there are no lumps.

CHANGE IT UP!

If you're vegetarian, use vegetable stock instead of chicken stock and add some lemon zest to replace the bacon.

1 Before starting, make sure that the frozen peas are fully defrosted. Put the peas, chicken stock, bread, 12 mint leaves, and lemon juice into a blender and pulse until smooth.

2 If the mixture is too thick, add up to 1 cup cold water and blend again until it reaches a souplike texture.

3 Stir in the crème fraîche and season with salt and pepper, then divide among 4 bowls.

4 Garnish with a few peas, the rest of the mint leaves, bits of crispy bacon, and a drizzle of olive oil. Serve with chunks of bread for dipping!

CAULIFLOWER RICE BOWL

30 mins

Serves 4

Rice bowls are usually made with sticky sushi rice. This version uses finely chopped cauliflower instead, which means you don't have to do any cooking!

TOOLS

- Mixing bowls
- Food processor
- Cutting board
- Sharp knife
- Dinner knife
- Vegetable peeler
- Spoons

INGREDIENTS

- 1 medium head of cauliflower
- ¼ cup rice vinegar
- 2 tsp sugar
- 2 avocados
- Juice of ½ a lime
- 4oz (120g) frozen edamame beans, defrosted
- 2 carrots, peeled and grated
- 8 radishes, thinly sliced
- 2 scallions, halved and thinly sliced
- 3½oz (100g) smoked salmon slices
- 2 nori (seaweed) sheets, torn into large pieces

TO SERVE

- 2 tsp sesame seeds
- Cilantro
- Lime wedges
- Soy sauce

TIP

See p. 14 for how to cut open an avocado and remove the pit safely.

1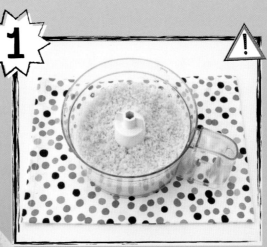

⚠️ To make the cauliflower rice, pull the leaves off the cauliflower. Carefully cut off the florets and throw away the thick stem. Put the florets in the food processor and pulse until they are a ricelike texture.

2 Pour into a mixing bowl and stir in the rice vinegar, sugar, and a pinch of salt. Put the cauliflower rice into 4 bowls.

3 ⚠️ Carefully cut open the avocados. Use a dinner knife to cut vertical lines into the flesh of each half—stop when you get to the peel.

4 Use a spoon to scoop out the avocado slices. Squeeze the lime juice over them—this will stop the avocado from going brown.

5 Arrange the edamame beans, avocado slices, grated carrot, radish slices, scallions, and smoked salmon on top of the rice in each bowl.

Serve immediately with lime wedges for squeezing and soy sauce for drizzling.

6 Tuck in some pieces of nori, then scatter the sesame seeds and cilantro over the top to serve.

TOOLS

- Cutting board
- Sharp knife
- Can opener
- Sieve
- Mortar and pestle
- Garlic press
- Mixing bowl
- Spoons
- Serving bowl
- Salad servers

INGREDIENTS

- 2 celery ribs, ends trimmed
- 3½oz (100g) Cheddar cheese, or other cheese
- ½ cucumber
- 3½oz (100g) radishes, tops trimmed
- 1 head of romaine lettuce, ends trimmed
- 14oz (400g) can of chickpeas
- ¾ cup macadamia nuts

FOR THE DRESSING

- ⅔ cup sour cream
- 2 tbsp mayonnaise
  ¼ tsp paprika
- 1 small garlic clove, crushed
- Juice of ½ a lemon
- 3 tbsp finely chopped chives

CHOPPED SALAD

15 mins,
plus resting

Serves 4

This creamy, vegetable-packed salad is an excellent way to practice your chopping skills.

1 Carefully cut the celery ribs in half lengthwise, then cut each half into small pieces, roughly ½ in (1 cm) thick.

2 Cut the cheese into cubes similar in size to the celery pieces.

3 Carefully slice the cucumber in half lengthwise, then use a teaspoon to scrape the seeds out of each half. Cut each half into 4 strips, then chop the strips into small pieces, roughly ½ in (1 cm) thick.

4 Carefully cut the radishes into pieces similar in size to the cucumber, then carefully slice the romaine lettuce into thin strips, roughly ½ in (1 cm) wide.

5 Open the can of chickpeas and drain using the sieve. Rinse well with cold water, then shake to get rid of any excess water. Pour the chickpeas into the serving bowl, along with all of the chopped vegetables.

6 Put the nuts in the mortar and pestle and crush until the biggest pieces are roughly the same size as the chickpeas, then transfer to the serving bowl.

7 Mix the dressing ingredients in a bowl with some salt and pepper. Pour into the serving bowl and toss with the salad servers—everything should be covered in dressing. Let stand for 20 minutes to allow the flavors to mix together, then serve.

CHANGE IT UP!

To make this dish vegetarian, don't use the anchovies in the dressing, swap out the chicken and bacon for sliced avocado, and use vegetarian Parmesan.

INGREDIENTS

- 2 precooked chicken breasts, shredded
- 2 romaine lettuce hearts, coarsely chopped
- 2oz (60g) Parmesan shavings
- 3 tbsp coarsely chopped chives
- 3 cups croutons
- 4 precooked bacon strips, coarsely chopped

FOR THE DRESSING

- 6 tbsp mayonnaise
- 1 tsp Dijon mustard
- 4 salted anchovy fillets, drained and patted dry
- ½ garlic clove, crushed
- Juice of 1 lemon

CHICKEN
CAESAR SALAD

Whip up this salad as a light lunch
or as a side dish for dinner. Yum!

25 mins   Serves 4

The anchovies in the dressing don't have a very strong flavor, but you can leave them out if you don't like the taste.

TOOLS

- Sharp knife
- Cutting board
- Garlic press
- Sieve
- Mini food processor
- Spoons
- Serving bowl
- Salad servers

1 ⚠️ To make the dressing, put all of the ingredients, except for the lemon juice, into the mini food processor. Blend until smooth.

2 Squeeze the lemon juice into the food processor. Add some cold water, so that the dressing can be thickly poured (the exact amount of water will depend on what mayonnaise you use).

3 Put all of the salad ingredients in a bowl. Drizzle the dressing over the top and toss everything together, so that the leaves are evenly coated. Serve right away, before the leaves become soggy!

49

15 mins

Serves 6

GAZPACHO

This colorful, cold vegetable soup comes from Spain. Grab some crusty bread to dip in it and cool down on a hot day!

TOOLS

- Mixing bowl
- Blender
- Spoons
- Vegetable peeler
- Liquid measuring cup
- Cutting board
- Sharp knife
- Serving bowls

INGREDIENTS

- 6oz (160g) stale baguette
- 1 cucumber, peeled and diced into cubes
- 2¼lb (1kg) ripe tomatoes, coarsely chopped
- 1 red bell pepper, coarsely chopped and seeded
- 1 green bell pepper, coarsely chopped and seeded
- 2 small garlic cloves
- 2 tbsp sherry vinegar
- ½ cup extra virgin olive oil, plus extra to drizzle
- 8 pitted black olives, to serve
- Handful of basil leaves, to serve

TIP
This is a great soup for a picnic. Chill it for a few hours in the fridge, then transfer to a thermos to take with you.

1 Tear the bread into coarse pieces. Fill the mixing bowl with cold water and briefly dunk each chunk of bread into it, just long enough so that it absorbs some water.

2 Lift the bread out and gently squeeze it to remove any excess water, then put into the blender.

3 Add most of the cucumber and chopped tomatoes, all of the bell peppers, the garlic cloves, sherry vinegar, and olive oil to the blender.

4 ⚠ Season with some salt and freshly ground black pepper, then puree until the soup is completely smooth. Divide the gazpacho into 6 bowls.

5 ⚠ Carefully slice the olives. Top the soup with the remaining cucumber and tomatoes, the olives, and the basil leaves. Finish with a drizzle of olive oil.

6 Eat right away, or don't add the toppings and store the soup in an airtight container in the fridge for up to 2 days.

15 mins,
plus soaking

Serves 4

COUSCOUS AND SPINACH SALAD

This recipe is delicious on its own, but is also excellent to serve with cooked meat or fish.

TOOLS

- Mixing bowl
- Liquid measuring cup
- Plate
- Spoons
- Fork
- Cutting board
- Sharp knife

INGREDIENTS

- ⅔ cup dry couscous
- ¾ cup water
- 1 red bell pepper
- 5½oz (150g) cherry tomatoes
- 2 large handfuls of spinach, finely chopped

TO SERVE

- 1 tbsp extra virgin olive oil
- Lemon wedges

1 Put the couscous in a mixing bowl with ¾ cup cold water. Cover with a plate and leave for about 30–40 minutes, or until the couscous has puffed up and all the water has disappeared.

2 Add a pinch of salt to the couscous, then use the fork to stir it well and fluff it up. Set aside.

3 ⚠ Carefully slice 4 sides off the red bell pepper and discard the leftover seeds and stem. Cut away any white parts from inside the bell pepper pieces, then slice into thin strips. Cut each strip into small cubes.

4 ⚠ Carefully cut the cherry tomatoes into quarters. Add them and the bell pepper cubes into the couscous bowl along with the spinach. Stir well to combine.

TO SERVE

Drizzle the olive oil on top, add salt and freshly ground black pepper, then mix everything together. Either cover and keep in the fridge for up to 12 hours, or serve immediately with the lemon wedges.

Grow in a
sunny place

Plant
in spring
to summer

GROW YOUR OWN
CARROTS

 **1** Carefully staple the trash bag inside the burlap bag. Next, poke a few holes at the bottom of the trash bag—this will help to drain away excess water.

 2 Fill the bag with potting mix and make shallow trenches in the top of the mix. Scatter the carrot seeds in the trenches, then cover with more potting mix.

 3 As the carrot plants grow, thin them out by pulling out about half of the plants—there should be a gap of roughly 2 in (5 cm) between each plant. This gives the plants space to grow.

 4 Water the carrot plants often and give them a liquid fertilizer once a week when the leaves begin to grow. They should be big and ready to wash and eat after about 12 weeks.

When you think of carrots, you probably picture orange vegetables. However, these pointed roots come in many different shapes and colors!

TOOLS

- Burlap bag
- Trash bag
- Stapler
- Carrot seeds
- Potting mix
- Liquid fertilizer

TIP
Use your carrots in these recipes.

Shrimp summer rolls pp. 82—83

Cauliflower rice bowl pp. 44—45

Sesame coleslaw p. 85

DIP POTS

These different colored dips are perfect for dunking nibbles, such as breadsticks and raw vegetables.

TOMATO HUMMUS

Makes 1¾ cups

INGREDIENTS

- 4oz (120g) semi-dried tomatoes, drained
- 14oz (400g) can of chickpeas, drained and rinsed
- ½ garlic clove, crushed
- 3 tbsp olive oil

1 ! Put all the ingredients in a food processor and pulse everything until smooth. Season with salt and pepper. Divide into ramekins and serve immediately.

CREAMY CHIVE DIP

Makes 1 cup

INGREDIENTS

- ½ cup mayonnaise
- ½ cup Greek yogurt
- Small handful of snipped chives

1 Mix all the ingredients together and season with salt and pepper. Spoon into ramekins and serve with thinly sliced vegetables and breadsticks.

TOOLS

- Food processor
- Spoons
- Scissors
- Garlic press
- Sieve
- Small glasses
- Ramekins

TO SERVE

- Basil leaves
- Thinly sliced vegetables, such as red bell peppers, cucumbers, and carrots
- Breadsticks

PEA AND BASIL PUREE

LAYERED DIPS

For a fun presentation, layer the dips in serving glasses.

1 Spoon a layer of each dip into a serving glass. Start with the pea and basil puree, then a thin layer of the chive dip, and finally the tomato hummus. Repeat for more serving glasses. Top with basil leaves and serve.

Makes 1¾ cups

INGREDIENTS

- 14oz (400g) frozen peas, fully defrosted
- 3 tbsp olive oil
- Large handful of basil leaves

1 ⚠ Put all the ingredients in a food processor and blend until you have a smooth puree. Season with salt and pepper. Spoon into ramekins and serve with vegetables and breadsticks.

INDIAN SHARING PLATTER

30 mins, plus soaking

Serves 4

The dishes here are inspired by Indian food. They are full of different flavors and textures and are made to be shared. Grab a bit of everything and dig in.

TOOLS

- Box grater
- Mixing bowls
- Mortar and pestle
- Liquid measuring cup
- Spoons
- Cutting board
- Sharp knife
- Serving bowls

TO SERVE

- Mango chutney
- Pomegranate seeds
- 2 handfuls of Bombay mix, coarsely crushed in a mortar and pestle
- Poppadoms

FOR THE SALAD

- ½ red onion, finely chopped
- Juice of 1 lemon
- Pinch of sugar
- ½ cucumber, diced
- 3 medium tomatoes, diced
- 1 tsp cumin seeds

1 Put the red onion and lemon juice in a bowl with the sugar and a pinch of salt. Stir and then let soak for 20 minutes.

2 Add the remaining ingredients to the bowl, mix well, then season with more salt and set aside.

FOR THE COCONUT PANEER

- ½ cup shredded, unsweetened coconut
- ¼ cup water
- 8 green cardamom pods
- 4oz (110g) paneer cheese, grated
- 1 tbsp black onion seeds
- ½ tsp turmeric
- Juice of 1 lime
- 2 scallions, thinly sliced
- Pinch of mild chili powder
- ½ tbsp sunflower oil
- 5 sprigs cilantro, coarsely chopped

1 Put the shredded coconut in a small bowl with ¼ cup water. Stir, then leave to soak for 20 minutes to fluff it up!

2 Once the coconut has soaked up all of the water, put the cardamom pods in the mortar and pestle. Grind them a couple of times to break the pods apart.

3 Using your fingers, pick out the black seeds from inside the pods and throw away the pods. Put the seeds back in the mortar and pestle and finely crush.

4 Mix together the crushed seeds and coconut with all the other ingredients. Season with a pinch of salt and set aside.

TO SERVE

Put everything in separate bowls on a large platter or the table. Add some of each dish to your plate and scoop up with poppadoms!

FOR THE RAITA

- ½ cucumber
- 1 cup whole-milk plain yogurt
- 20 mint leaves, coarsely chopped

1 ⚠ Carefully slice the cucumber in half lengthwise, then drag a teaspoon along the seeds to scoop them out.

2 Grate the cucumber into a bowl. Spoon in the yogurt, then stir in the mint leaves. Mix together and set aside.

59

CREPE SPIRALS

25 mins · **Makes 24**

These nectarine, ricotta, and honey bites are so easy to make. Make sure you roll them up tightly so the filling doesn't fall out!

TOOLS

- Sharp knife
- Cutting board
- Dinner knife
- Spoons

INGREDIENTS

- 2 nectarines
- 4 crepes, premade
- 4 tbsp ricotta cheese
- 4 tsp honey

1 ⚠

Use the sharp knife to cut carefully down each side of the nectarine, until you're left with large pieces and the pit. Cut each chunk into thin slices and throw away the pit. Repeat for the other nectarine.

2

Leave some room at the top and bottom of the crepe to help you roll it.

Lay a crepe on the cutting board and spread over 1 tbsp of ricotta cheese. Arrange some nectarine slices on top (about half a nectarine per crepe) then drizzle 1 tsp of honey on top.

3 ⚠

Starting at the bottom, roll up the crepe as tightly as you can, being careful not to rip it. Once it's rolled up, carefully slice the top and bottom off to straighten the ends, then cut into 6 equal pieces.

4

Repeat steps 2 and 3 with the remaining crepes, then enjoy! You can cover and keep these fruit-filled spirals in the fridge for up to 1 day.

FRUIT AND CHEESE SKEWERS

These yummy skewers are packed full of flavor—they are both sweet and savory.

TOOLS

- Cocktail skewers
- Sharp knife
- Cutting board
- Mortar and pestle
- Spoons

15 mins

Each recipe makes 6

WATERMELON, FETA, AND PEANUT

INGREDIENTS

- 2oz (60g) feta cheese, cut into 6 cubes
- 6 mint leaves
- 4oz (120g) watermelon, cut into 6 triangles
- 1 tbsp salted peanuts, to serve

1 Thread each cube of feta cheese onto a cocktail skewer. Fold 1 mint leaf on each stick. Finish each skewer with a watermelon triangle.

2 Put the peanuts in the mortar and pestle and crush them coarsely. Arrange the skewers on a plate, then sprinkle the crushed peanuts over the top and serve immediately.

APPLE, CHEDDAR, AND GRAPE

INGREDIENTS

- 2oz (60g) Cheddar cheese
- ½ apple
- 6 red grapes
- 1 sprig of thyme, leaves stripped, to serve

1 Carefully cut the Cheddar cheese into 6 cubes and slice the apple half into 6 wedges.

2 Thread a grape, followed by a cube of cheese, and then an apple wedge onto each cocktail skewer. Arrange on a plate, scatter the thyme leaves on top. Serve immediately.

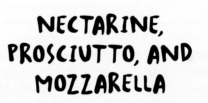

NECTARINE, PROSCIUTTO, AND MOZZARELLA

INGREDIENTS

- 6 mini mozzarella cheese balls
- 6 basil leaves
- 2 slices prosciutto
- 1 nectarine

1 Push a mozzarella ball onto each cocktail skewer, then add a basil leaf.

2 Tear each slice of prosciutto into 3 pieces. Fold each piece 2–3 times so they're roughly the same size as the mozzarella balls, then thread those on.

3 Use a sharp knife to cut the nectarine in half, remove the pit with a teaspoon, then cut each half into 3 wedges.

4 Thread the nectarine wedges onto the cocktail skewers. Serve immediately.

NUTTY RED BELL PEPPER PUREE

This bright orange dish is a simple snack with a nutty flavor. It comes from Spain and is great to dip fresh vegetables in, or you can spread it on crackers.

20 mins Serves 6–8

TOOLS

- Food processor
- Cutting board
- Sharp knife
- Sieve
- Liquid measuring cup
- Spoons
- Paper towels
- Garlic press

TIP
Any leftovers can be kept in a sealed container in the fridge for up to 4 days, or they can be frozen—make sure the puree is defrosted completely before serving.

INGREDIENTS

- 16oz (460g) jar roasted red bell peppers, drained and patted dry
- 1 small garlic clove, crushed
- 3½oz (100g) stale baguette
- ¼ tsp paprika, plus extra to serve
- ¼ tsp sugar
- 1 cup toasted, sliced almonds
- ¾ tbsp sherry vinegar
- ⅓ cup extra virgin olive oil, plus extra to drizzle

TO SERVE
- Vegetable batons
- Cucumber, diced
- Radishes, diced
- Handful of basil leaves
- Crackers

CHANGE IT UP!
In addition to a dip and spread, this is a tasty paste to add to grilled chicken or fish.

1 ⚠️ Put the bell peppers, garlic, bread, paprika, sugar, almonds, and vinegar in the food processor with a good pinch of salt. Pulse until it reaches a creamy paste texture.

2 ⚠️ Slowly pour in the olive oil and puree until the mixture is smooth and thick.

3 If you're using it as a dip, scrape the puree into a serving bowl. Use the back of a teaspoon to create a swirl on the surface. Drizzle over a little more olive oil and a sprinkle of paprika. Serve with your choice of vegetables.

4 If you're topping crackers, spread a little of the bell pepper puree on top of the cracker, then scatter over some finely diced cucumber and radishes and some small basil leaves. Eat right away, so the crackers don't get soggy!

30 mins,
plus draining

Serves 4

DUKKAH AND LABNEH

TOOLS

- Spoons
- Cheesecloth, or finely woven dish towel
- Kitchen twine
- Kitchen scissors
- Mortar and pestle
- Mixing bowl
- Sieve
- Serving bowls
- Jar with lid

Dukkah is a finely crushed mix of spices, nuts, and salt that comes from Egypt. It's a tasty snack when combined with creamy labneh, which is strained yogurt. Dukkah can also be used to season meat.

1 To make the dukkah, put all of the ingredients in the mortar and pestle. Pound them for a few minutes, until finely ground. Transfer to a serving bowl or a jar—the dukkah will keep for up to 3 weeks in an airtight container.

INGREDIENTS

FOR THE DUKKAH

- ⅓ cup roasted, chopped hazelnuts
- ⅓ cup toasted, sliced almonds
- 2 tsp cumin seeds
- 1 tsp ground coriander
- 2 tbsp sesame seeds
- 1 tsp kosher salt

FOR THE LABNEH

- 2¼ cups whole-milk Greek yogurt
- 2 large pinches of salt

TO SERVE

- Bread
- Olive oil
- Vegetables

DUKKAH

A sprinkle of dukkah will give the Nectarine and feta salad on pp. 32—33 an extra crunch!

TO SERVE

Spread the labneh on some bread, sprinkle the dukkah over the top, and drizzle with some olive oil.

LABNEH

Chop up some vegetables to dip into the labneh then dukkah.

1 To make the labneh, open the yogurt, pour away any liquid that has gathered on the top, add the salt, and stir well.

2

Lay the cloth flat, then scoop the yogurt into the middle of it. Gather the four corners of cloth, and tie tightly with string to make a bag shape.

3

Put the bag in a sieve set over a mixing bowl. The excess liquid will drip away. Leave it in the fridge, still in the sieve over the mixing bowl, for 24 hours before unwrapping.

4 Scoop the labneh into a serving bowl—it should be thick and creamy. Eat right away, or cover and keep in the fridge—it will stay fresh for up to 4 days.

ALMOND BUTTER DIP

This is a nutty and sweet alternative to savory dips. It's easy to make as a snack or to pack in a lunchbox.

CHANGE IT UP!
You can replace the almond butter with the same amount of peanut butter.

15 mins,
plus soaking

Serves 4

TOOLS

- Spoons
- Mixing bowl
- Sieve
- Small food processor
- Serving bowl

INGREDIENTS

- 5 medjool dates, pits removed
- ¼ cup almond butter
- 2 tbsp plain Greek yogurt
- ½ tsp vanilla extract
- Squeeze of lemon juice
- Roasted, chopped hazelnuts, to garnish
- Sliced apples and pears, to serve
- Strawberries, to serve

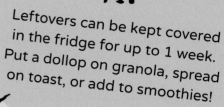

TIP

Leftovers can be kept covered in the fridge for up to 1 week. Put a dollop on granola, spread on toast, or add to smoothies!

 1 Put the dates in the mixing bowl and cover with cold water. Leave to soak and soften for up to 30 minutes.

 2 Take out 1 tbsp of the water and set aside, then drain the dates using the sieve.

 3 ⚠ Put the dates, the water you set aside, and all of the remaining dip ingredients, except for the hazelnuts, in the small food processor. Pulse until completely smooth.

 4 Scoop into a serving bowl, scatter some chopped hazelnuts over the top, and serve with fresh fruit for dipping.

SOAKED OLIVES

Plain olives can become a really yummy snack, just by letting them sit and soak up the flavors of other ingredients.

10 mins, plus marinating

Each recipe makes 7oz (200g)

TOOLS

• Cutting board
• Sharp knife
• Spoons
• Airtight containers

LEMON AND FETA

INGREDIENTS

• 1–2 preserved lemons
• 2oz (60g) feta cheese
• 2 tsp cumin seeds
• 5½oz (150g) pitted black olives (1 heaping cup)
• ¼ cup olive oil

1 ⚠️ Slice each lemon in half and then into quarters. Carefully cut the flesh away from the lemon peel and throw away. Slice the peel into thin strips.

2 ⚠️ Coarsely chop the feta cheese into chunks.

3 Put the feta cheese, lemon peel, and the rest of the ingredients in an airtight container. Stir together, then leave covered in the fridge for at least 6 hours before enjoying the dish.

INGREDIENTS

- 2 sprigs of rosemary, leaves picked
- 4 sprigs of thyme, leaves picked
- 2 tsp fennel seeds
- 5½oz (150g) pitted mixed green and black olives (1 heaping cup)
- ¼ cup olive oil

HERB AND FENNEL

1 Mix all the ingredients together in an airtight container. Stir well, then leave to sit and soak in the fridge for at least 6 hours before you dive in.

TIP

All of these will keep for up to 2 days in an airtight container in the fridge. Once you eat the olives, you can use the leftover oil in salad dressings.

GARLIC AND CHILI

INGREDIENTS

- 6 garlic cloves
- 1 tsp dried oregano
- Small pinch of chili flakes
- 5½oz (150g) pitted green olives (1 heaping cup)
- ¼ cup olive oil

1 See p. 18 for how to peel the garlic cloves. Put the peeled garlic in an airtight container with the other ingredients and stir.

2 Keep covered in the fridge for at least 6 hours to help the flavors infuse together. Serve with a big pinch of freshly ground black pepper.

Grow in a
cool place

Plant
in spring

GROW YOUR OWN
SPINACH

This plant's green leaves and stems are full of vitamins and minerals. Spinach helps you stay healthy and grow big and strong.

TOOLS

- Long container
- Potting mix
- Ruler
- Spinach seeds
- Liquid fertilizer
- Scissors

1

Fill the long container with potting mix. Use the ruler to make a trench about 1 in (2.5 cm) deep all along the potting mix. Sprinkle the spinach seeds in the trench, then cover with more potting mix.

2 As the spinach grows, remove some leaves to thin the plants out a bit—there should be a gap of roughly 3 in (8 cm) between each plant.

3 Water often, and use liquid fertilizer once a month. Trim any small shoots when they grow from the larger leaves.

4 When any leaves get longer than 2 in (5 cm), cut them off to wash and then eat!

TIP

Use your spinach in these recipes.

Spinach pesto zucchini p. 81

Couscous and spinach salad pp. 52—53

Green goodness smoothie p. 24

You can substitute the same amount of smoked trout for the mackerel.

TIP

Both the pâté and beet slaw can be made one day ahead of serving—just keep them covered in the fridge.

SMOKED FISH PÂTÉ

Pâté comes from France, and it is a paste that is often made from ground meat. This one, though, is made from smoked, salted fish.

20 mins, plus marinating

Serves 2–3

 To make the slaw, carefully grate the beets into a mixing bowl. Stir in the remaining ingredients until everything is combined. Set aside to marinate (soak together) for up to 30 minutes.

 To make the pâté, peel the skin off the mackerel fillets. Use your hands to break the fillets up into pieces, then place the pieces in a mixing bowl.

 Add the sour cream and lemon juice to the mackerel and mash with a fork until there are no big pieces of fish left. Mash until everything is mixed together.

 Stir in the parsley, then either scoop the pâté into ramekins or put large spoonfuls onto plates.

 Drain the slaw in a sieve to get rid of any extra liquid. Divide among the plates, then serve with crackers. Enjoy!

TOOLS

- Mixing bowls
- Box grater
- Spoons
- Fork
- Sharp knife
- Cutting board
- Vegetable peeler
- Sieve
- Ramekins or plates

INGREDIENTS

FOR THE BEET SLAW

- 7oz (200g) raw beets, peeled and tops trimmed
- Juice of ½ a lemon
- 1 tsp sugar
- Large pinch of salt
- ½ tbsp olive oil

FOR THE PÂTÉ

- 8oz (230g) boneless smoked mackerel
- ¼ cup sour cream
- Squeeze of lemon juice
- ¼ cup coarsely chopped parsley
- Crackers, to serve

SHRIMP
BUTTER POTS

Before refrigerators were invented, mixing shrimp with butter was one way to keep them from spoiling. It's also a very tasty way to eat them—especially when the butter is flavored with herbs, spices, and lemon.

30 mins, plus chilling

Serves 4

TIP

If you don't have ground mace, you can use ground nutmeg.

TOOLS

- Electric mxer
- Liquid measuring cup
- 4 ramekins or small jars, each with 4oz (100ml) capacity
- Mixing bowls
- Sieve
- Microplane
- Vegetable peeler
- Plastic wrap
- Spoons

INGREDIENTS

- 10½ tbsp unsalted butter
- Large pinch of cayenne pepper
- Large pinch of ground mace
- Zest of ½ a lemon
- 3 tbsp finely chopped chives
- 5oz (140g) small, precooked shrimp (preferably Gulf shrimp), drained
- Whole-wheat crusty bread, to serve

FOR THE PICKLED CUCUMBER

- ½ a cucumber
- ¼ cup white wine vinegar
- 1½ tbsp sugar
- ¼ tsp fine salt

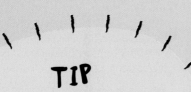

1 Leave the butter out at room temperature for a few hours until it's really soft to the touch. Put it in a mixing bowl.

2 ⚠ Add the cayenne pepper, ground mace, lemon zest, chives, and a large pinch of salt to the bowl. Beat with the electric mixer for 1–2 minutes, or until the mixture turns a pale color and has a soft, fluffy texture.

3 Stir in the shrimp using a spoon. Once everything is mixed together, divide among the ramekins or jars. Cover with plastic wrap and refrigerate overnight.

4 The next day, take the shrimp pots out of the fridge about 30 minutes before serving so that the mixture can soften. Meanwhile, use the vegetable peeler to peel ribbons of cucumber.

5 Put the cucumber in a mixing bowl with the vinegar, sugar, and salt and toss to coat. Let stand for 20 minutes, stirring halfway through.

6 Once the ribbons have softened, drain in a sieve and gently squeeze to get rid of any extra liquid.

TO SERVE

Serve the shrimp pots with a handful of pickled cucumbers and some whole-wheat bread. The shrimp pots will keep covered in the fridge for up to 3 days.

ZUCCHINI NOODLES

Use a spiralizer to make zucchini noodles that look very similar to spaghetti. But unlike spaghetti, zucchini noodles don't need to be cooked—just add a tasty sauce and enjoy a healthy dinner.

20 mins   Serves 4

TOOLS

- Cutting board
- Sharp knife
- Spiralizer
- Scissors

FOR THE ZUCCHINI NOODLES

- 4 zucchini, halved with ends trimmed

 1 See p. 14 for how to use a spiralizer. Take extra care when using one—they can be quite sharp. Use it to cut the zucchini—you should end up with a big tangle of noodles. Repeat for the remaining zucchini.

 2 If the noodles are longer than normal spaghetti, use scissors to trim them. Use the zucchini as soon as you've spiralized it—it doesn't keep very well and can become soft.

 3 Choose one of the three sauces on this page or the next, coat the zucchini noodles, twirl them around your fork, then enjoy!

CHANGE IT UP!

If you don't have a spiralizer, a julienne peeler is a great alternative and will produce thin zucchini noodles.

CREAMY AVOCADO AND PARMESAN

5 mins

Serves 4

TO SERVE
- Small mint leaves
- Sprinkle of chili flakes

TOOLS

- Cutting board
- Sharp knife
- Food processor
- Mixing bowl
- Garlic press
- Microplane
- Spoons

INGREDIENTS

- 2 ripe avocados
- 1½oz (40g) Parmesan cheese, grated, plus extra to serve
- Juice of 1 lemon, plus the grated zest to serve
- 1 garlic clove, crushed
- 2 tbsp extra virgin olive oil, plus extra to serve
- Zucchini noodles

1 See p. 14 for how to cut open an avocado and remove the pit. Repeat for the second avocado.

2 Using a spoon, scoop the flesh out from each avocado half, then put it in the food processor. Add the Parmesan cheese, lemon juice, crushed garlic, olive oil, and a pinch of salt.

3 Pulse everything until it's completely smooth, then taste and add more salt if you think the recipe needs it.

4 Put the zucchini in a bowl and pour the sauce over the top. Using your hands, toss everything together until the noodles are completely coated in the sauce. It might be messy work, but it's worth it!

5 Divide among 4 bowls. Top with some lemon zest, a few mint leaves, chili flakes, if you can handle the spice, and, finally, a drizzle of olive oil.

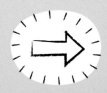

10 mins, plus
marinating

Serves 4

TOOLS

- Cutting board
- Sharp knife
- Mixing bowl
- Spoons

INGREDIENTS

- 4oz (120g) feta cheese
- 1¼lb (500g) tomatoes, coarsely chopped
- 2 tsp red wine vinegar
- Large pinch of sugar
- 2 tbsp extra virgin olive oil, plus extra to serve
- Zucchini noodles (p. 78)
- 1 tsp dried oregano

1 Use your hands to break the feta cheese into chunks and set aside. Put the tomatoes, vinegar, sugar, olive oil, and a pinch of salt in the mixing bowl.

2 Stir everything together, then let soak for 15–20 minutes so that the tomatoes soften and release tasty juices into the bowl.

3 Add the zucchini noodles to the mixing bowl and toss together with the tomato mixture. Stir in the feta cheese chunks and oregano. Divide among 4 bowls, then twist it all up and eat!

SIMPLE TOMATO

SPINACH PESTO

10 mins   Serves 4

TOOLS

- Food processor
- Mixing bowl
- Spoons
- Garlic press

INGREDIENTS

- 3½oz (100g) spinach leaves
- 1½ cups fresh basil leaves, plus extra to serve
- ½ cup pine nuts
- 1 garlic clove, crushed
- 3 tbsp olive oil
- 1¾oz (50g) Parmesan cheese, grated, plus extra to serve
- Zucchini noodles (p. 78)

1 Put all of the ingredients, except for the noodles, into the food processor with a generous helping of salt and freshly ground pepper. Pulse until the pesto is smooth.

2 Place the zucchini noodles in the mixing bowl and spoon in the pesto. Use your hands to coat the noodles.

3 Divide among 4 bowls and top with some basil leaves and a little more grated Parmesan—add as much as you like.

30 mins   Makes 5

SHRIMP
SUMMER ROLLS

These mouthwatering rolls are inspired by Vietnamese flavors and are filled with fresh vegetables, herbs, and shrimp. They are both fun to make and scrumptious to eat!

INGREDIENTS

- 1 carrot, peeled
- ⅓ cucumber
- 5 little gem lettuce leaves
- 5 rice paper wrappers
- 5½oz (150g) precooked jumbo shrimp
- 20 mint leaves
- 2 scallions, thinly sliced lengthwise

FOR THE DIPPING SAUCE

- 3 tbsp peanut butter
- 1 tsp soy sauce
- 2 tsp fish sauce
- 1 tsp sugar
- Juice of ½ a lime
- ½ garlic clove, crushed
- 2 tbsp water

TOOLS

- Julienne peeler
- Frying pan
- Spoons
- Mixing bowl
- Cutting board
- Dish towel
- Scissors
- Garlic press

Don't forget to dip the rolls in the sauce!

1 ⚠ Carefully drag the julienne peeler down the length of each side of the carrot so you get lots of little strands. Stop when you reach the carrot's core.

 2 ⚠ Repeat with the cucumber, stopping when you reach the seeds. Snip the lettuce leaves into thin slices.

 3 Divide the vegetables into 5 piles, each with slices of carrot, cucumber, and lettuce. Stir all of the sauce ingredients together and set aside.

 4 Fill a frying pan with cold water. Dip a rice paper wrapper into it for 1–2 minutes, until it becomes completely softened.

 5 Once the wrapper is soft, lift it out of the pan very carefully—try not to let it fold in on itself. Gently lay it down on a clean dish towel.

These summer rolls will keep in the fridge, wrapped in plastic wrap, for 1 day.

 6 Line up 4 shrimp across the middle of the wrapper, then top with 4 mint leaves, some scallion, and one of the vegetable piles.

7

Carefully cover the filling with the bottom of the wrapper.

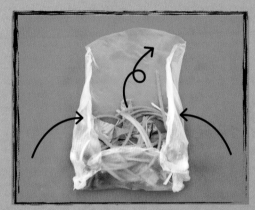

Fold both sides of the wrapper inward. Finally, gently roll it all up as tightly as you can.

8 Transfer to a plate. Repeat steps 4–7 until you have 5 rolls in total. Serve with the dipping sauce.

COLESLAW
THREE WAYS

20 mins, plus marinating

Each recipe serves 4

Coleslaw is made with cabbage, carrot, and onion. You can add the extra ingredients here for different flavors—or choose your own!

INGREDIENTS

- ¼ white cabbage, finely chopped
- 1 large carrot, grated
- ½ red onion, thinly sliced

TOOLS

- Cutting board
- Sharp knife
- Mixing bowl
- Spoons
- Box grater

This coleslaw is yummy at barbecues.

 To make the coleslaw base, put the white cabbage, carrot, and red onion in the mixing bowl. Stir in the extra ingredients needed for whichever coleslaw you choose to make.

 Cover and chill for at least 30 minutes, or overnight, so the flavors can soak into the vegetables.

CLASSIC COLESLAW

INGREDIENTS

- 1 tbsp mayonnaise
- 1 tbsp whole-milk plain yogurt
- Squeeze of lemon juice

1 Mix everything together in a bowl with some salt, then pour over the coleslaw base and toss until coated.

APPLE COLESLAW

This coleslaw is delicious when eaten with slices of cheese and cooked ham.

INGREDIENTS

- 1 apple
- 4 sprigs of parsley, leaves finely chopped
- 1 tbsp whole-grain mustard
- 2 tsp red wine vinegar

1 ⚠️ Use a sharp knife to carefully cut down each side of the apple, until you're left with four large pieces and the core. Cut each piece into thin strips and throw away the core.

2 Mix the apple and parsley into the coleslaw base, then stir in the mustard, red wine vinegar, and a pinch of salt. Toss until coated.

SESAME COLESLAW

This tangy coleslaw goes well with the Chicken and mango boats on pp. 94—95, or the Shrimp summer rolls on pp. 82—83.

INGREDIENTS

- 1 tbsp toasted sesame oil
- 2 tbsp sesame seeds
- Juice of 1–2 limes

1 Mix all of the ingredients together in a bowl and add a pinch of salt. Pour on top and coat the coleslaw base.

CHANGE IT UP!

This sauce also goes well with cooked chicken, or any type of smoked fish, such as mackerel or trout.

Keep any leftover sauce in a sealed jar in the fridge for up to 5 days.

TIP

If you're not sure about the mustard flavor, add half of the mustard first, then the rest at the end if you like it.

SWEET MUSTARD AND DILL SAUCE

This sweet and sharp sauce is creamy and pairs perfectly with smoked salmon. Enjoy at breakfast, lunch, or dinner!

TOOLS

- Spoons
- Whisk
- Mixing bowl
- Liquid measuring cup
- Scissors

INGREDIENTS

- 1 egg yolk
- 1 tbsp white wine vinegar
- 1 tbsp Dijon mustard
- ½ tbsp sugar
- ⅔ cup sunflower oil
- 3 tbsp finely snipped fresh dill
- Juice of ½ a lemon

TO SERVE

- 4 slices of whole-wheat bread, buttered and cut into triangles
- 7oz (200g) smoked salmon
- Lemon wedges

Please note: the finished recipe contains uncooked egg.

1 Put the egg yolk, vinegar, mustard, and sugar in a medium mixing bowl with a large pinch of salt. Whisk for 1–2 minutes until everything is combined and has a pale color.

Slowly pour in the oil while continuously whisking. (You can ask someone to pour while you mix.) The mixture should thicken up a little.

Make sure you add the oil in a slow stream, not all at once.

3 Once all the oil has been mixed in, stir in the dill and then taste the sauce. If it needs a bit more sharpness, squeeze in some lemon juice.

4 Arrange the bread triangles and smoked salmon on 4 plates. Drizzle the sauce over the salmon and serve with lemon wedges.

PANZANELLA

30 mins, plus soaking

Serves 4

This salad comes from Italy and is an excellent way to use up any stale bread you have, such as the leftover bread from the Muffuletta on pp. 30–31. The juices from the tomatoes and bell peppers soak into the bread, making it soft and chewy.

TOOLS

- Cutting board
- Sharp knife
- Mixing bowl
- Spoons
- Salad servers

INGREDIENTS

- 2 red bell peppers
- 2¼lb (1kg) ripe tomatoes
- 3 tbsp capers
- 4 tsp red wine vinegar
- ¼ cup extra virgin olive oil, plus extra for drizzling
- ½ tsp sugar
- 10oz (300g) very stale bread
- 2 handfuls of basil leaves
- 2 medium balls mozzarella cheese

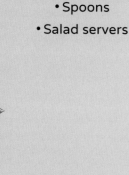

1 Carefully slice the four sides off each red bell pepper and throw away the leftover seeds and stem. Cut away any white parts from inside the bell pepper pieces. Chop the bell peppers into coarse chunks.

2 Coarsely chop the tomatoes. They should be a similar size to the chunks of red bell pepper.

3 Put the bell peppers, tomatoes, and capers in the mixing bowl. Add a pinch of salt, then set aside for about 10 minutes—the juices will start to come out of the tomatoes.

4 Mix together the vinegar, olive oil, and sugar. Pour this mixture over the tomatoes, bell peppers, and capers, then toss everything together with the salad servers.

5 Tear the bread into pieces, then stir it into the mixing bowl. Allow the panzanella to sit for about 20–30 minutes, stirring it every now and then, until the bread is soft and has soaked up the juices.

6 Stir in the basil leaves, then divide among 4 bowls. Tear each mozzarella ball in half, then place a half in each bowl. Drizzle with a little more olive oil. Add a pinch of salt and freshly ground black pepper, then dig in!

TACO FEAST

These make-your-own tacos are full of different flavors. Put all of the dishes on the table so that everyone can choose their favorites.

FOR THE MASHED AVOCADO

- 2 ripe avocados
- Juice of ½ a lime, plus extra to taste
- Large bunch of cilantro

1 ⚠️ See p. 14 for how to cut open an avocado and remove the pit. Repeat for the second avocado.

2 Use a spoon to scoop out the flesh from each avocado half. Put this in a mixing bowl with the lime juice and a pinch of salt.

3 Snip the cilantro into the bowl. Set aside some leaves (you'll need them for the corn salsa!). Mash together, then taste. If you think the mix needs more sharpness, squeeze in extra lime juice.

FOR THE CHICKEN

- 2 precooked chicken breasts, shredded
- 4 medium tomatoes, diced
- 1 tsp ground cumin
- ¼ tsp paprika
- ¼ tsp ground coriander
- 1 tsp dried oregano
- Drizzle of olive oil
- Large bunch of cilantro, coarsely chopped

1 Mix all of the ingredients together, then season generously with salt and freshly ground black pepper.

TO SERVE

Get out the sour cream, grated cheese, lime wedges, and tacos. Give everyone a plate, then wrap up your tacos!

Mashed avocado

Sour cream

Chicken

TOOLS

40 mins   **Serves 4**

- Small food processor
- Cutting board
- Sharp knife
- Scissors
- Spoons
- Mixing bowls
- Can opener
- Sieve
- Garlic press

TO SERVE

- Sour cream
- Grated cheese of your choice
- Lime wedges
- Soft corn tacos

FOR THE BEAN DIP

- 14oz (400g) can of red kidney beans, drained
- 3 tbsp olive oil
- 1 garlic clove, crushed
- ½ tsp ground cumin
- ¼ tsp ground cinnamon
- Juice of ½ a lemon
- Pinch of paprika, plus extra to serve

1 ⚠️ Put all of the ingredients in a small food processor with 3 tbsp water and pulse until smooth.

2 Season with salt and pepper, then scoop into a serving bowl and sprinkle paprika on top.

FOR THE CORN SALSA

- ½ red onion, finely chopped
- Juice of 2 limes
- 1 tsp sugar
- 1 red bell pepper, finely chopped and seeded
- 7oz (200g) can of corn, drained

1 Mix the onion with lime juice, a pinch of salt, and the sugar in a mixing bowl. Set aside for 10 minutes to soak, then add the rest of the ingredients.

2 Coarsely chop the cilantro you set aside to make the mashed avocado. Stir the leaves into the corn salsa.

3 Season with another pinch of salt, then put on the table and start building your tacos.

Don't forget about your favorite cheese!

Bean dip

Corn salsa

Wrap everything together in soft corn tacos.

SEAFOOD HAND ROLLS

Japanese hand rolls are often filled with rice and other ingredients, but you can also make them with just vegetables and seafood sticks. Roll them the right way, and you *should* be able to eat them with one hand!

 **1** Start by preparing your vegetables. Carefully cut the cucumber in half lengthwise, then use a teaspoon to scrape out the seeds. Cut into long, thin batons and set aside.

 2 Carefully slice the 4 sides off the red bell pepper and discard the seeds and stem. Cut away any white parts from inside the bell pepper, then slice into long, thin batons.

 3 Trim the root off the lettuce and gently pull the leaves off. Cut the leaves lengthwise into thin strips. Put the cucumber, bell pepper, lettuce, and sprouts on a plate.

 4 Take a nori sheet and lay it flat on a clean, dry surface. The smooth side of the nori sheet should be facing downward.

CHANGE IT UP!
To make this vegetarian, replace the seafood sticks with avocado slices.

25 mins

Makes 5

TOOLS

- Sharp knife
- Cutting board
- Dinner knife
- Spoons
- Plate

INGREDIENTS

- ⅓ cucumber
- 1 red bell pepper
- 1 little gem lettuce
- Handful of bean sprouts
- 10 seafood sticks
- 5 chives
- 5 rectangular nori (seaweed) sheets

TO SERVE

- Black or white sesame seeds
- Juice of ½ a lime
- Sweet chili sauce, to drizzle

5

When rolling, start from the bottom left-hand corner.

Place one-fifth of the vegetables on the left-hand side of the nori, arranged diagonally. Put 2 seafood sticks and a chive folded in half on top.

6

Dampen this edge.

Roll the nori around the filling so it forms a cone. Once rolled, wet your fingers and dampen the nori—stick it to the cone to secure the roll. Repeat to make 4 more hand rolls.

To serve, scatter some sesame seeds and squeeze some lime juice over the filling. Drizzle with sweet chili sauce.

DID YOU KNOW?

Nori is a type of edible seaweed often used in Japanese cooking. The seaweed is pounded into sheets and then dried.

93

CHICKEN AND MANGO BOATS

Lettuce leaves are great for holding fillings. They are also easy to roll up and eat. These crunchy salad bites are full of flavor—they are sweet, sour, salty, and a little bit spicy!

INGREDIENTS

- ⅓ cup salted peanuts
- 1 ripe mango
- 2 precooked chicken breasts, shredded
- Juice of 1 lime
- 3 mint sprigs, coarsely chopped
- Large bunch of cilantro, coarsely chopped
- 2 tbsp sweet chili sauce
- 1 tsp fish sauce
- 1–2 little gem lettuces

TOOLS

- Mortar and pestle
- Sharp knife
- Cutting board
- Dinner knife
- Spoons
- Mixing bowls

20 mins

Makes 16

1 ⚠️ Put the peanuts in the mortar and pestle and grind them up until they're finely crushed. Carefully cut down the sides of the mango, avoiding the pit.

3 Use a spoon to scoop out the flesh. The mango will be in small cubes. Put them in a bowl with the peanuts and shredded chicken, then mix it all up. Stir in the rest of the ingredients, except the lettuce.

2

Once scored, your mango should have lots of little squares on it.

Lay the cut mango skin-side down on the cutting board. Use the dinner knife to score thin lines down and across the flesh, stopping when you reach the peel.

4 ⚠️ Trim the root off the lettuce, then gently pull the leaves off one by one, trimming more off the root when needed. You'll need 16 leaves in total. Divide the filling among the lettuce boats and you're finished!

RAW PIZZA

This recipe has all of the flavors of a pizza, without any of the baking! We've topped ours with slices of pepperoni, mozzarella cheese, and fresh tomatoes, but you can get creative and use whatever toppings you like.

15 mins

Makes 4

TIP

Use flatbreads for this recipe, not premade pizza crusts.

TOOLS

- Mini food processor
- Cutting board
- Pizza cutter
- Spoons

INGREDIENTS

- 4 flatbreads

FOR THE SAUCE

- 6oz (180g) semi-dried tomatoes, drained
- 1oz (35g) mascarpone
- Handful of basil leaves, plus extra to serve

TO TOP EACH PIZZA

- 5 slices of pepperoni
- 6 mini mozzarella cheese balls, halved
- 3 cherry tomatoes, halved

CHANGE IT UP!

You can also use the sauce to make pizza wraps! Spread 1 tbsp of the sauce on a soft tortilla wrap. Add the pizza toppings, then roll up the wrap. Any remaining sauce will keep covered in the fridge for up to 1 week. This sauce is also delicious stirred into cooked pasta or as a dip for breadsticks and vegetables.

1 ! To make the sauce, put the semi-dried tomatoes, mascarpone, and basil in the mini food processor. Pulse until you have a smooth sauce.

2 Spoon 2 tbsp of the sauce onto each flatbread. Use the back of the spoon to spread the sauce out—make sure you leave a small gap around the edges so you have a crust!

3 Top with pepperoni slices, mozzarella cheese, tomatoes, and the extra basil leaves.

4 ! To serve, use the pizza cutter to cut each flatbread into quarters. Fold each quarter in half and use your hands to dig in!

ZUCCHINI AND TUNA SALAD

This salad has a creamy dressing and is packed with tons of flavor. The butter beans make it really filling, so you can have it on its own for lunch or dinner.

TOOLS

- Vegetable peeler
- Sharp knife
- Can opener
- Cutting board
- Sieve
- Mixing bowls
- Spoons
- Bowls

20 mins, plus marinating

Serves 3–4

INGREDIENTS

- 1 large zucchini
- Juice of ½ a lemon
- 14oz (400g) can of butter beans, drained and rinsed
- 3½oz (100g) radishes, thinly sliced
- 6oz (160g) can of tuna in brine, drained

FOR THE DRESSING

- ¼ cup crème fraîche
- Juice of ½ a lemon
- 3 tbsp finely chopped chives
- 1 tsp olive oil

1 Carefully slice both ends off the zucchini, then drag the vegetable peeler lengthwise along the zucchini to make ribbons—stop when you get to the seeds (you can throw those away).

 2 Put the zucchini ribbons in a bowl, squeeze the lemon juice on top, and sprinkle in a pinch of salt. Use your hands to coat the zucchini ribbons. Leave to soften for up to 10 minutes.

 3 Meanwhile, make the dressing by stirring all of the ingredients together in a bowl. Season with salt and pepper and set aside.

 4 Once the ribbons have softened, squeeze them gently to release any liquid. Remove the extra liquid from the bowl. Add the butter beans and sliced radishes. Pour in the dressing and toss everything together.

 5 Put the tuna into the bowl, making sure to break up any large chunks. Stir the salad one last time—be gentle so you don't break up the tuna too much. Plate it and dig in!

Grow in a
sunny place

Plant
in the fall
or spring

GROW YOUR OWN
STRAWBERRIES

1 Fill the medium pot with soil. Leave a small hole in the middle of the soil. Put the strawberry plug in the hole, then cover the bottom of the plug with soil. Water well.

2

To stop the strawberries from touching the ground, add some straw to cover the soil. This will lift up your growing strawberries.

These bright red fruits should be planted somewhere where there is no wind. They will be ready to enjoy in the summer sunshine.

TOOLS

- Strawberry plug
- Medium pot
- Soil
- Straw
- Liquid fertilizer

3 This plant needs to be watered every day. Start giving it liquid fertilizer every 10 days once the strawberries start to grow.

4 Once any strawberries turn red, pick them right away. Keep the plant well watered to help the strawberries grow big and juicy. Wash before eating!

TIP
Use your strawberries in these recipes.

Berry and cherry oatmeal p. 23

Eton mess semifreddo p. 123

FRUIT PARFAITS

15 mins, plus chilling

Makes 4

Nothing beats a creamy fruit parfait on a hot day. They can be made with whatever fruit you have at home. We've used berries and plums, but you can try out your own flavor combinations!

TOOLS

- Sharp knife
- Cutting board
- Liquid measuring cup
- Mixing bowl
- Spoons
- Sieve
- Electric mixer
- 4 serving glasses
- Plastic wrap

INGREDIENTS

- 2 plums
- ⅔ cup heavy cream
- 1 cup whole-milk Greek yogurt
- 1 tsp pure vanilla extract
- 2 tbsp confectioners' sugar
- 3 tbsp berry compote, or jam
- 2 ginger cookies, to serve

1 Begin by preparing your plums. Using the sharp knife and the cutting board, carefully cut down each side of the plum, until you're left with 4 large pieces and the pit.

2 Cut each chunk into small pieces and throw away the pit. Repeat for the other plum. Set aside.

3 Put the heavy cream, yogurt, and pure vanilla extract into the mixing bowl. Use the sieve to sift in the confectioners' sugar.

4 Beat the mixture for 1–2 minutes with the electric mixer until it forms soft, shiny peaks. Don't beat too much, or it will become grainy. The peaks should flop over when you lift the beaters out.

5 Add 3 tablespoons of the berry compote into different places in the cream. Carefully fold the compote into the cream, until you have a swirled effect—don't stir it in completely.

6 Divide half of the plum pieces among 4 glasses, then pour in some of the whipped cream. Top with the remaining plums, then the rest of the whipped cream.

7 Chill in the fridge for up to 30 minutes. Cover with plastic wrap if leaving in the fridge overnight. When ready to eat, crumble over the cookies. Ta-dah!

CHOCOLATE POWER BALLS

These chewy little bites are excellent energy-boosting snacks between meals.

 30 mins, plus chilling

 Makes 14

TOOLS

- Food processor
- Plates
- Plastic wrap
- Spoons
- Mortar and pestle

INGREDIENTS

- 1 cup pecan halves
- 4 dates, pits removed
- ½ cup shredded, unsweetened coconut
- 3 tbsp almond butter, or other nut butter
- 4 tsp cocoa powder
- 1 tbsp maple syrup
- 1 tbsp vegetable oil
- ¼oz (10g) freeze-dried strawberries

 1 Put the pecans in the food processor and pulse until finely crushed.

 2 Put the remaining ingredients, except for the freeze-dried strawberries, in the food processor. Pulse everything until it's smooth.

 3 Using your hands, roll the mixture into small balls, then put on a plate—you should end up with 14 balls. Cover with plastic wrap and chill for 1 hour.

 4 Finely crush the freeze-dried strawberries in the mortar and pestle—they should turn into a powder.

 5 Now decorate! Dip a ball into the strawberry powder so you coat half of it. Repeat for the remaining balls.

 6 Transfer your chocolate power balls to an airtight container and chill until you want one. These will keep in the fridge for up to 2 weeks, but are so tasty they might not last that long!

RASPBERRY RIPPLE FRIDGE CAKE

This is one of the easiest cakes you'll ever make. Take your time building up the cookie tower, before demolishing the whole thing and diving in!

CHANGE IT UP!

You can choose any type of cookie you'd like, flavor the whipped cream with maple syrup or elderflower, and decorate with different toppings!

25 mins, plus chilling

Serves 10–12

TOOLS

- Mixing bowl
- Liquid measuring cup
- Electric mixer
- Spoons
- Fork

INGREDIENTS

- 1¼ cups heavy whipping cream
- 1 cup whole-milk Greek yogurt
- 2 tsp pure vanilla extract
- 3 tbsp confectioners' sugar
- 8oz (225g) raspberries
- 15–20 jam-filled cookies

TIP

Try and make sure the ingredients are evenly layered as you go.

1 Put the whipping cream, yogurt, pure vanilla extract, and confectioners' sugar in a bowl. Beat with the electric mixer for 2–3 minutes, until the mixture forms soft peaks. The mixture will flop over when you lift the beaters out.

2

Crush 3½oz (100g) of the raspberries in a bowl with a fork. Spoon them into the whipped cream mixture and gently fold together.

3

Put 6 cookies in a circle on the cake plate, then place 1 more in the center of the circle. Cover with some of the whipped cream mixture.

Scatter some of the remaining raspberries between each layer of whipped cream.

4 Arrange 4 more cookies in a circle on top of the whipped cream. Cover with more whipped cream and raspberries.

5 Top with a triangle of 3 cookies and cover with the remaining whipped cream and raspberries.

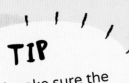

6 Balance the final cookie on top, then transfer to the fridge for at least 30 minutes, or up to 12 hours.

MINI TRIFLES

The best thing about a trifle is the tasty filling—layers and layers of it. Choose your favorite flavor or mix-and-match.

10 mins, plus chilling

Each recipe makes 4

TOOLS

- Mixing bowls
- Spoons
- Freezer bag
- Rolling pin
- Sharp knife
- Cutting board
- Serving glasses
- Can opener

TO SERVE

If eating right away, top each trifle with canned whipped cream, then sprinkle on the toppings. Or, don't add the toppings, and cover and refrigerate for up to 12 hours.

INGREDIENTS

- 1 cup vanilla yogurt
- ¼ cup chocolate spread
- 8 graham crackers
- 7oz (200g) raspberries
- Canned whipped cream, to serve
- 4 tbsp mini marshmallows, to top

1 Put the yogurt in a mixing bowl and add in the chocolate spread. Swirl it into the yogurt using a spoon, then set aside.

2 Crumble the graham crackers into large pieces, then divide half of the pieces among 4 glasses.

3 Crush the raspberries with your fingers and divide half of them among the glasses. Top with the yogurt mix, then add the rest of the cracker pieces and berries.

S'mores are snacks filled with melted chocolate and marshmallows. They are usually eaten around a campfire—this trifle has the flavor, but none of the fire!

S'MORES

INGREDIENTS

- 8 ginger cookies, plus crumbs to top
- 4 bananas, peeled and sliced
- 6 tbsp caramel sauce
- 1 cup vanilla yogurt
- Canned whipped cream, to serve

 Put the cookies in the freezer bag. Close the bag, then bash gently with the rolling pin until the cookies are coarsely crushed.

 Divide half of the crushed cookies among 4 glasses, then put half of the banana slices in each glass.

 Pour the caramel sauce into each glass. Put a dollop of the yogurt on top, then add the rest of the cookies and bananas.

Make sure your bananas are nice and ripe, with speckled peels.

BANOFFEE

INGREDIENTS

- 4oz (120g) sponge cake, crumbled into small pieces
- 12 peach slices from a can, coarsely chopped, plus the juice
- ½ cup strawberry jelly
- ¾ cup ready-made custard
- Canned whipped cream, to serve
- Sweet popcorn, to top
- Sprinkles, to top

 Divide the cake pieces among 4 glasses and press down on them with your fingers. Pour 1 tbsp of the peach juice into each glass for the cake to soak up.

Divide the chopped peaches among the glasses. Top with the jelly and custard.

This trifle is full of fruit, jelly, and custard. We've topped it with crunchy popcorn and sprinkles!

PEACHES AND CREAM

WATERMELON SLUSH

**15 mins,
plus freezing**

Makes 4

This ice-cold drink is zingy and fruity. It's easy to make and you can swap out the watermelon for other melon if you like.

TOOLS

- Blender
- 2 pint (1 liter) freezer-proof container
- Fork
- 4 glasses
- Spoons
- Paper straws, lime wedges, and cocktail umbrellas (optional)

INGREDIENTS

- 2lb (900g) watermelon, peeled carefully, cut into quarters, seeded, and cut into chunks (see p. 7 "Kitchen safety" for how to cut a large fruit with a thick rind)
- 1 tbsp sugar
- Juice of 1 lime

1 Put all of the ingredients in the blender and puree until the mixture is a smooth juice. Pour into the freezer-proof container and freeze for 1–2 hours.

2 After 1–2 hours, remove from the freezer and scrape the fork through the mixture, breaking up any pieces that have frozen solid.

3 Put the container back in the freezer and repeat step 2 each hour for the next 4–5 hours, or until the mixture becomes a frozen slush.

4 When you are ready to serve it, allow the slush to melt at room temperature for 5–10 minutes. Pour into glasses and decorate with colorful straws, lime wedges, and tiny umbrellas, if you like.

CHANGE IT UP!
You can use cantaloupe or honeydew melon instead, but add a splash of water when blending.

BLACK FOREST
BANANA SPLITS

If you can't get frozen cherries, try frozen berries instead.

Inspired by the chocolate and cherry flavors of a Black Forest cake, these banana splits are made with instant ice cream. Add yogurt to frozen fruit and watch it magically transform before your eyes!

20 mins, plus freezing

Makes 4

TOOLS

- Spoons
- Food processor
- Freezer-proof container
- Ice cream scoop
- Dinner knife
- Bowl
- Cutting board

INGREDIENTS

- 14oz (400g) pitted frozen cherries
- 1 cup whole-milk Greek yogurt
- 2 tbsp golden syrup (or honey)
- 4 bananas
- Canned whipped cream
- 12 fresh cherries
- Chocolate sauce and sprinkles, to serve

1 To make the ice cream, put the frozen cherries, yogurt, and golden syrup (or honey) in the food processor. Blend until it reaches a smooth ice-cream texture.

2 Pour the mixture into a freezer-proof container and freeze for at least 2½ hours.

3 When ready to serve, take the ice cream out of the freezer. If it's too solid, leave it out at room temperature to soften a little.

4 Meanwhile, peel, then carefully slice the bananas in half lengthwise. Place 2 halves in a bowl, then top with 2 scoops of ice cream, some whipped cream, 3 fresh cherries, a drizzle of chocolate sauce, and sprinkles.

TIP

You can keep any leftover ice cream covered in the freezer for up to 1 week.

113

APPLE DOUGHNUTS

30 mins

Makes 8

There's no dough in these "doughnuts"—just lots of fruits, flavors, and crunchy nuts.

INGREDIENTS

- 2 apples
- 4 tsp peanut butter, or other nut butter
- 4 tsp chocolate spread

TO TOP
- Dried fruit, such as raisins or chopped apricots
- Sprinkles (chocolate or multicolored)
- Freeze-dried raspberries or strawberries, coarsely crushed
- Chopped nuts, such as hazelnuts or pecans
- Shredded, unsweetened coconut

TOOLS

- Sharp knife
- Cutting board
- Apple corer
- Paper towels
- Spoons

This one is topped with peanut butter and sprinkles. Yum!

Get creative with toppings! You can use anything you like.

1 ⚠ Carefully cut the top and bottom off each apple, then use the apple corer to remove both cores.

2 ⚠ Cut each apple horizontally into 4 pieces, so that you end up with 4 rings per apple. Use paper towels to blot each ring to dry its surface a little.

3 Spread peanut butter on 4 rings and chocolate spread on the other 4. Scatter toppings of your choice over the top, then chomp away!

115

NO-BAKE CRUMBLES

10 mins

Makes 6 crumble bases

Serve these fruity crumbles with custard or ice cream. You can mix and match fillings and toppings to find the combinations you like best.

TIP

The crumble base will keep in an airtight container somewhere cool and dry for up to 5 days.

TOOLS

- Food processor
- Spoons
- Airtight container

FOR THE CRUMBLE BASE

- 2oz (50g) speculoos cookies, or other spiced cookies
- 1oz (25g) pretzels (about 4 twists)
- 1 cup low-sugar granola
- 2 tbsp maple syrup

1 Put the cookies, pretzels, and granola into the food processor. Pulse until everything is finely crushed, but has a bread-crumblike texture.

2 Divide your choice of filling among 6 bowls. Stir the maple syrup into the crumble topping just before you add it to the fruit, to stop it from becoming soggy.

PLUM AND RASPBERRY

25 mins,
plus soaking

Makes 6

TOOLS

- Box grater
- Spoons
- Mixing bowl
- Serving bowls
- Juicer
- Plastic wrap

INGREDIENTS

- 12oz (350g) plums, coarsely chopped
- 12oz (350g) raspberries
- 2 tsp brown sugar
- Juice of 1 lemon

FOR THE TOPPING

- 4½oz (125g) marzipan, grated
- ¼ tsp ground cinnamon

1 Put the fruit in the mixing bowl. Scatter the sugar on top and squeeze in the lemon juice.

2 Stir together, then cover with plastic wrap and let sit for 1 hour—the sugar and lemon will draw the juices out of the fruit and soften everything up.

3 Sprinkle the marzipan and cinnamon directly into the crumble base from the previous page. Once the fruit is ready, divide into 6 bowls, then scatter the crumble topping over the fruit.

Here are 2 more types of
crumble for you to try.
Grab a spoon and dig in!

25 mins,
plus soaking

Makes 6

TOOLS

- Sharp knife
- Cutting board
- Spoons
- Serving bowls
- Mixing bowl
- Juicer
- Plastic wrap

INGREDIENTS

- 12oz (350g) strawberries, halved
- 12oz (350g) blueberries
- 2 tsp brown sugar
- Juice of 1 lemon

FOR THE TOPPING

- ⅔ cup milk chocolate chips
- ⅓ cup roasted, chopped hazelnuts

STRAWBERRY AND BLUEBERRY

1 Put the strawberries and blueberries in the mixing bowl, then add the sugar and lemon juice. Stir together, then cover with plastic wrap and let sit for 1 hour.

2 Mix the chocolate chips and hazelnuts into the crumble base from p. 116. Once the fruit is ready, divide into 6 bowls, then add the crumble topping. Share it with five lucky friends!

INGREDIENTS

- 12oz (350g) pineapple chunks
- 12oz (350g) mango chunks
- 2 tsp brown sugar
- Juice of 1 lime

FOR THE TOPPING

- ½ cup shredded, unsweetened coconut
- Zest of 1 lime

25 mins, plus soaking

Makes 6

TOOLS

- Spoons
- Serving bowls
- Mixing bowl
- Microplane
- Plastic wrap

TIP

Zest the lime before you juice it—it's much easier to zest a plump, whole lime.

PINEAPPLE AND MANGO

1 Put the pineapple and mango in the mixing bowl, then sprinkle the sugar on top. Pour in the lime juice.

2 Mix well, then cover with plastic wrap and set aside for 1 hour.

3 Mix the shredded coconut and lime zest into the crumble base from p. 116. When the fruit has softened, put into 6 bowls, then top with the crumble topping.

4 Serve with ice cream or custard—coconut ice cream is especially nice!

119

Line the loaf pan with plastic wrap so the sides are covered. You'll need to leave enough plastic wrap hanging over the sides of the pan to cover the top of the semifreddo.

 See p. 16 for how to separate egg yolks and whites. Put the yolks into a mixing bowl with the sugar. Using the electric mixer, beat them for 2–3 minutes, until the mixture is airy and pale in color.

 Mix in the creamed coconut and most of the lime zest until combined with the egg yolks.

 Clean the beaters, then put the cream, yogurt, and lime juice into another mixing bowl. Beat until you have soft peaks. Set aside.

SEMIFREDDOS

A semifreddo is an Italian ice-cream cake!
It's super creamy and melts in your mouth.
Turn the page to see more flavors to make.

FOR THE LIME, GINGER, AND COCONUT

- 2 large eggs
- ¼ cup sugar
- 1¾oz (50g) sachet of creamed coconut
- Zest and juice of 2 limes
- ½ cup heavy whipping cream
- ½ cup whole-milk Greek yogurt
- 6 ginger cookies, coarsely crushed
- Toasted coconut flakes, to serve

Please note: the finished recipe contains uncooked egg.

TOOLS

- 1lb (450g) loaf pan
- Plastic wrap
- Electric mixer
- Mixing bowls
- Spatula
- Microplane
- Spoons
- Plate
- Liquid measuring cup

30 mins, plus freezing

Serves 6–8

Clean the beaters again, then put the egg whites into another mixing bowl. Beat for 2–3 minutes, until stiff peaks form.

 Use a metal spoon to fold the whipped cream into the egg yolk mixture—be careful not to knock the air out. Fold in one spoonful of the egg whites until everything is mixed.

 Gently fold in the remaining egg whites—only add a little at a time, until everything is smooth and airy. The mixture will be very loose.

 Carefully fold in most of the crushed cookies, then spoon the mix into the loaf pan. Cover the top with plastic wrap, then freeze for at least 12 hours, or up to 1 week.

Remove the plastic wrap, then scatter the remaining crushed cookies on top. Sprinkle on the rest of the lime zest and coconut flakes to decorate.

TIP
To make the creamed coconut easy to mix, put the sachet in warm water for 15–20 minutes.

TO SERVE
Take out of the freezer and leave for 15–20 minutes. Put a plate on top of the pan, then flip them both over together. The semifreddo should fall out—tug the plastic wrap if it doesn't.

FOR THE APRICOT AND PISTACHIO

- 2 large eggs
- ¼ cup sugar
- 1 tsp pure vanilla extract
- ½ cup heavy whipping cream
- ½ cup whole-milk Greek yogurt
- 5 tbsp apricot compote, or jam
- ⅓ cup pistachios, coarsely crushed
- 1 apricot, sliced, to serve

* Please note: the finished recipe contains uncooked egg.

TOOLS

- 1lb (450g) loaf pan
- Plastic wrap
- Electric mixer
- Mixing bowls
- Spatula
- Spoons
- Mortar and pestle
- Metal spoon
- Sharp knife
- Cutting board

 30 mins, plus freezing

 Serves 6–8

1 Repeat step 1 from p. 120.

2 Repeat step 2 from p. 120, but add the vanilla extract.

3 Repeat steps 4–7 from pp. 120–121, but don't add the lime juice in step 4.

4 Fold in the apricot compote or jam and most of the pistachios. Spoon into the loaf pan. Cover with the plastic wrap and freeze.

5 Follow the "To serve" instructions on p. 121.

6 Remove the plastic wrap, then arrange the apricot slices and the remaining pistachios on top.

FOR THE ETON MESS

- 2 large eggs
- ¼ cup sugar
- 1 tsp pure vanilla extract
- 5½oz (150g) strawberries
- 5½oz (150g) raspberries
- 1 tbsp confectioners' sugar
- ½ cup heavy whipping cream
- ½ cup whole-milk Greek yogurt
- 8 mini meringues

* Please note: the finished recipe contains uncooked egg.

TOOLS

- 1lb (450g) loaf pan
- Plastic wrap
- Electric mixer
- Mixing bowls
- Spatula
- Spoons
- Mortar and pestle
- Metal spoon
- Sharp knife
- Cutting board
- Fork

30 mins, plus freezing

Serves 6–8

The name of this semifreddo comes from a traditional English dessert, made with cream, berries, and meringue.

 1 Repeat step 1 from p. 120.

 2 ⚠ Repeat step 2 from p. 120, but add the vanilla extract.

 3 ⚠ Repeat steps 4–7 from pp. 120–121, but don't add the lime juice in step 4.

 4 Put 3½oz (100g) each of the strawberries and raspberries and all the sugar into a bowl. Use the fork to crush together.

 5 Fold the crushed berries into the semifreddo mixture and crumble in 6 meringues. Spoon into the loaf pan. Cover with the plastic wrap and freeze.

 6 Follow the "To serve" instructions on p. 121. Remove the plastic wrap, then crumble over the rest of the meringues and top with the leftover berries.

123

GLOSSARY

BEAT
Evenly mix ingredients together using an electric mixer

BLEND
Mix ingredients together in a blender or food processor until combined

CHILL
Cool in the fridge, or keep cool

CHOP
Use a knife to cut ingredients into smaller pieces

CITRUS
Sharp flavor of citrus fruits, such as lemons and limes

COMBINE
Mix ingredients together evenly

CREPE
Thin pancake

DICE
Cut ingredients into small, equal cubes

DRAIN
Remove liquid from something and let it flow somewhere else, such as into a sink

DRIZZLE
Pour slowly, in a trickle

FLORET
Small, flower-shaped piece of a vegetable, such as cauliflower

FOLD
Mix ingredients together gently without knocking out the air

GARNISH
Toppings added to a dish before serving

GRATE
Shred ingredients into little pieces by rubbing them against a grater

GRIND
Crush ingredients until they become a fine powder

JUICE
Squeeze the liquid out of fruits or vegetables

MARINATE
Soak food in other ingredients so it can develop a certain flavor

PITTED
Food that has had its pit removed

PORTION
Amount or helping of food

PUREE
Thick pulp, usually of fruits or vegetables

RINDLESS
Without an outer skin, such as rindless goat cheese

SEASON
Add salt, pepper, herbs, or spices to food

SLICE
Use a knife to cut food into strips

SUBSTITUTE
Change one ingredient for another

TEXTURE
Way an ingredient feels when you touch or taste it. For example, it could be smooth or rough

THICKEN
When a liquid becomes stiffer and more solid

VARIATION
Another option to prepare the recipe, either with different ingredients or a different way of presenting the dish

WHISK
Evenly mix ingredients together with a handheld whisk

INDEX

A

almond butter
  almond butter dip 68–69
  chocolate power balls 104–105
apples
  apple coleslaw 85
  apple doughnuts 114–115
apricot and pistachio semifreddo 122
arugula
  brie, pear, and arugula picnic
  baguette 40
avocados
  avocado spread 34–35
  cauliflower rice bowl 44–45
  creamy avocado and Parmesan 79
  removing pits 14
  taco feast 90–91

B

bacon
  chicken Caesar salad 48–49
baguettes, picnic 40–41
bananas
  banoffee trifles 109
  Black Forest banana splits 112–113
bean dip 91
beating 16
beet slaw 74–75
bell peppers
  gazpacho 50–51
  muffuletta 30–31
  nutty red bell pepper puree 64–65
  panzanella 88–89
berry and cherry oatmeal 23
Black Forest banana splits 112–113
blueberries
  fall oatmeal 23
  strawberry and blueberry crumble 118
bread
  avocado spread 34–35
  muffuletta 30–31
  panzanella 88–89
  picnic baguettes 40–41
breakfast smoothies 24–25

C

cabbage
  coleslaw three ways 84–85
Caesar salad, chicken 48–49

carrots
  coleslaw 84–85
  growing 54–55
cauliflower rice bowl 44–45
cheese
  brie, pear, and arugula picnic
  baguette 40
  chicken Caesar salad 48–49
  chickpea and tomato salad 36–37
  chopped salad 46–47
  fruit and cheese skewer 62–63
  Indian sharing platter 58–59
  lemon and feta olives 70
  muffuletta 30–31
  nectarine and feta salad 32–33
  panzanella 88–89
  raw pizza 96–97
  simple tomato zucchini noodles 80
cherries
  berry and cherry oatmeal 23
  Black Forest banana splits 112–113
chicken
  chicken and mango boats 94–95
  chicken Caesar salad 48–49
  coronation chicken picnic
  baguette 41
  taco feast 90–91
chickpeas
  chickpea and tomato salad 36–37
  chopped salad 46–47
  tomato hummus 56
chive dip, creamy 56
chocolate power balls 104–105
chocolate spread
  apple doughnuts 114–115
  s'mores trifles 108–109
citrus fruit
  juicing 16
  zesting 17
coleslaw 84–85
corn salsa 91
cookies
  no-bake crumbles 116–117
  raspberry ripple fridge cake 106–107
coronation chicken picnic baguette 41
couscous and spinach salad 52–53
cream
  fruit parfaits 102–103
  mini trifles 109
  raspberry ripple fridge cake 106–107
  semifreddo 120–121

crepe spirals 60–61
crumbles, no-bake 116–119
cucumber
  gazpacho 50–51
  pickled cucumber 76–77
  raita 59
curry
  coronation chicken picnic baguette 41
custard
  peaches and cream trifles 109

D

dips 56–57, 64–65, 68–69, 91
drinks 24–25, 110–111
dukkah 66

E

edamame beans
  cauliflower rice bowl 44–45
egg yolks and whites, separating 16
Eton mess semifreddo 123

F

fall oatmeal 23
fish
  cauliflower rice bowl 44–45
  smoked fish pâté 74–75
  zucchini and tuna salad 98–99
flatbreads
  raw pizza 96–97
folding 17
fridge cake, raspberry ripple 106–107
fruit
  fruit and cheese skewers 62–63
  fruit parfaits 102–103

G

gardening equipment 10–11
garlic, crushing 18
gazpacho 50–51
granola, no-bake 20–21
graters 15

HIJ

ham
  muffuletta 30–31
herbs 18
hummus, tomato 56

hummus, tomato 56
Indian sharing platter 58–59
jeweled oatmeal 22
juicing citrus fruit 16

KL

knives, how to use 13
labneh 66–67
lettuce
  chicken and mango boats 94–95
  chicken Caesar salad 48–49
  growing 38–39

M

mangos
  chicken and mango boats 94–95
  jeweled oatmeal 22
  pineapple and mango crumble 119
mayonnaise
  creamy chive dip 56
meringues
  Eton mess semifreddo 123
microplane, zesting with a 17
mint pea soup 42–43
muffuletta 30–31
mustard
  sweet mustard and dill sauce 86–87

NO

nectarines
  crepe spirals 60–61
  nectarine and feta salad 32–33
nori
  seafood hand rolls 92–93
nuts
  chopped salad 46–47
  dukkah 66
  no-bake granola 20–21
oatmeal, overnight 22–23
olives, soaked 70–71

P

paneer
  Indian sharing platter 58–59
panzanella 88–89
pâté, smoked fish 74–75
peaches and cream trifles 109
peanut butter
  apple doughnuts 114–15
  peanut butter sauce 82
pears
  brie, pear, and arugula picnic baguette 40
  fall oatmeal 23
peas
  mint pea soup 42–43
  pea and basil puree 57
peelers 12

pesto
  muffuletta 30–31
  spinach pesto zucchini noodles 81
pickled cucumber 76–77
picnic baguettes 40–41
pineapple and mango crumble 119
pistachios
  apricot and pistachio
  semifreddo 122
pizza, raw 96–97
plants, growing 11
plum and raspberry crumble 117
pomegranate seeds
  jeweled oatmeal 22
power balls, chocolate 104–105

R

raita 59
raspberries
  Eton mess semifreddo 123
  plum and raspberry crumble 117
  raspberry ripple fridge cake 106–107
  s'mores trifles 108–109
ricotta
  pancake spirals 60–61

S

salads
  chicken Caesar salad 48–49
  chickpea and tomato salad 36–37
  chopped salad 46–47
  coleslaw 84–85
  zucchini and tuna salad 98–99
  couscous and spinach salad 52–53
  Indian sharing platter 58–59
  nectarine and feta salad 32–33
  panzanella 88–89
salami
  muffuletta 30–31
salsa, corn 91
sandwiches
  muffuletta 30–31
  picnic baguettes 40–41
seafood hand rolls 92–93
semifreddos 120–123
shrimp
  shrimp cocktail picnic
  baguette 40–41
  shrimp summer rolls 82–83
shrimp butter pots 76–77
skewers, fruit and cheese 62–63
slaw, beet 74–75
slush, watermelon 110–111
smoked salmon
  cauliflower rice bowl 44–45
smoothies 24–25
  smoothie bowls 26
  smoothie pops 27

soups
  gazpacho 50–51
  mint pea soup 42–43
spinach
  couscous and spinach salad 52–53
  growing 72–73
  spinach pesto zucchini noodles 81
spiralizers 14
strawberries
  Eton mess semifreddo 123
  growing 100–101
  strawberry and blueberry crumble 118
summer rolls, shrimp 82–83

T

taco feast 90–91
techniques 12–13
tomatoes
  avocado spread 34–35
  chickpea and tomato salad 36–37
  couscous and spinach salad 52–53
  gazpacho 50–51
  growing 28–29
  Indian sharing platter 58–59
  muffuletta 30–31
  panzanella 88–89
  raw pizza 96–97
  simple tomato zucchini noodles 80
  taco feast 90–91
  tomato hummus 56
tools 6, 8–11, 13, 14–15, 17
trifles, mini 108–109
tuna
  zucchini and tuna salad 98–99

VW

vegetable ribbons and julienne strips 12
watermelon slush 110–111

YZ

yogurt
  banoffee trifles 109
  Black Forest banana splits 112–113
  creamy chive dip 56
  Eton mess semifreddo 123
  fruit parfaits 102–103
  labneh 66–67
  mini trifles 108–109
  overnight oatmeal 22–23
  raita 59
  raspberry ripple fridge cake 106–107
  semifreddo 120–121
zesting 17
zucchini
  zucchini and tuna salad 98–99
  zucchini noodles 78–81
zucchini noodles 79

ACKNOWLEDGMENTS

The author would like to thank: Katie Lawrence and the team at DK for their help and support (especially during the trials of testing during lockdown!); her son, Henry, who was an incredibly enthusiastic guinea pig, and her husband, Oliver, for eating uncooked meals every day for a month and being nice about all of them. Thanks also to Jess Meyer—recipe tester and assistant extraordinaire—for taking the time to style each one of the recipes beautifully for the test shots. A simple gesture but very much appreciated!

DK would like to thank: Vanessa Bird for the index; Laura Nickoll for proofreading; Lynne Murray for picture library assistance; James Mitchem for editorial advice; and Anne Damerell for legal assistance.

The publisher would like to thank the following for their kind permission to reproduce their photographs:

(Key: a-above; b-below/bottom; c-center; f-far; l-left; r-right; t-top)

10 Dreamstime.com: Airborne77 (br); Catherine Eckert (cb); Christophe Testi (cra); Penchan Pumila / Gamjai (cr); Alexander Pladdet / Pincarel (bc/ Garbage bag); Anton Starikov (bl, bc, crb). **11 Dreamstime.com:** Airborne77 (bl); AntonStarikov (clb). **15 123RF.com:** Karandaev (crb). **28 Dreamstime.com:** Marian Pentek Digihelion. **29 Dreamstime.com:** Dusan Kostic (cr). **59 Dreamstime.com:** Philip Kinsey (ca). **100-101 Dreamstime.com:** Maljalen (c)

All other images © Dorling Kindersley
For further information see: www.dkimages.com